Also by Eric Henze

The Complete Guide to Wilder Ranch State Park

Grand Circle Travel Guide Series

    A Family Guide to the Grand Circle National Parks

    Top Trails of Utah

    Top Trails of Arizona

    Top Trails of Nevada

    Top Trails of Colorado and New Mexico

    RVing with Monsters

All titles published by Gone Beyond Guides

Find us on Facebook and Twitter!

 facebook.com/GBG.GoneBeyondGuides

 twitter.com/GoneBeyondGuide

THE COMPLETE GUIDE TO
HENRY COWELL REDWOODS STATE PARK

Eric Henze

Gone Beyond Guides
Publisher

Copyright 2015-2016, Eric Henze, Gone Beyond Guides. Unless otherwise noted, product names, designs, logos, titles, text, images, audio and video within this book are the trademarks, service marks, trade names, copyrights or other intellectual property (collectively, "Intellectual Property") of Eric Henze and Gone Beyond Guides. All other unregistered and registered trademarks are the property of their respective owners. See Attributions for full list of credits.

No Warranties; Limitation of Liability.

THIS CONTENT IS PROVIDED "AS IS" AND "WITH ALL FAULTS" WITHOUT WARRANTIES OF ANY KIND WHATSOEVER, WHETHER EXPRESS, IMPLIED, BY OPERATION OF LAW OR OTHERWISE INCLUDING, WITHOUT LIMITATION, IMPLIED WARRANTIES OF MERCHANTABILITY, FITNESS FOR A PARTICULAR PURPOSE, NON-INFRINGEMENT OR OTHERWISE.

All photos used in this book are either the work of the author, within public domain or available for commercial reuse through one or more of the following licenses: GNU Free Documentation License, version 1.2, NPS Copyright policy, under the Creative Commons Attribution-Share Alike 3.0 Unported, 2.5 Generic, 2.0 Generic and 1.0 Generic license as indicated in Attributes section of book.

You can reach the author through our FaceBook page: www.facebook.com/GBG.GoneBeyondGuides

ISBN-10: 0989039285

ISBN-13: 978-0-9890392-8-4

To finding someone you feel has been with you the whole time...

Contents

ACKNOWLEDGEMENTS XI
INTRODUCTION 1
GENERAL INFORMATION 2
   GETTING THERE 2
   GAS, FOOD, LODGING 3
   OPERATING HOURS, AMENITIES AND TELEPHONE 4
   CAMPING 4
   FEES 6
   HANDICAP ACCESSIBILITY 6
   DOGS, HORSES, HIKERS AND MOUNTAIN BIKES 7
   WEATHER BY SEASON AND RECOMMENDED CLOTHING . 8
   WHAT TO DO, SEE AND KNOW 9
PARK HISTORY 10
   NATIVE PEOPLE 10
   THE MEXICAN RANCHOS 13
      Rancho Carbonera 13
      Rancho Zayante 15
      Rancho Cañada del Rincon en el Rio San Lorenzo 18
   CALIFORNIA POWDER WORKS 20
   CAPTAIN ISAAC GRAHAM 22
      Birth, Early Days as a Trapper 22
      Indian Attack in the Rockies 23
      Graham First Arrives in California 24
      The Graham Affair 25
      California's First Power Sawmill and Final Years 29

HENRY COWELL	31
The Brother's Cowell Head West	31
Lime Builds a Strong Business Empire	32
Henry Cowell – The Person	35
The Fateful Year of 1903	36
Son Ernest Takes Over the Business	37
Final Years under Samuel Harry Cowell	38
WELCH'S BIG TREE GROVE	40
Catalyst of the First State Park	40
Andrew Putnam Hill	41
The End Story of Welch's Big Tree Grove	42
JOHN FRÉMONT	43
GEOLOGY	**46**
TRAILS IN THE MAIN UNIT	**48**
TRAILS AROUND THE ENTRANCE AND MAIN PARKING	53
North Big Trees Park Road	53
Meadow Trail	55
Redwood Grove Loop Trail	57
River Trail	59
Zayante Trail	61
Pipeline Road	65
TRAILS CLOSER TO THE SAN LORENZO RIVER (WEST HALF)	67
Ox Fire Road/Ox Trail	67
Rincon Fire Road	69
Diversion Dam Trail	71
Big Rock Hole Trail	73
Buckeye Trail	75
TRAILS CLOSER TO THE CAMPGROUND (EAST HALF)	77
Eagle Creek Trail	77
Powder Mill Fire Road	79
Pine Trail	81
Columbine Trail	83
Ridge Fire Road	85
Powder Mill Trail	87
Graham Hill Trail	89
TRAILS IN THE FALL CREEK UNIT	**91**
TRAILS OF THE SOUTHERN PORTION	91
Bennett Creek Trail	95
Fall Creek Fire Road	97
Fall Creek Trail	99
Kiln Fire Road	103

  High School Trail 105
  Ridge Trail 107
  S-Cape Trail 109
  South Fork Trail 113
 TRAILS OF THE MID AND NORTHERN PORTION 115
  Lost Empire Road 115
  Truck Trail 117
  Big Ben Trail 119
  Sunlit Trail 121
  Pine Flat Trail 123
  Old Alba Road 125

FLORA 126
 SANTA CRUZ SANDHILLS CHAPARRAL PLANTS 127
  Bonny Doon Manzanita (*Arctostaphylos silvicola*) 127
  Knobcone pine (*Pinus attenuata*) 128
  (Sticky Monkey) Bush monkeyflower (*Mimulus aurantiacus*) 128
  Wartleaf Ceanothus (*Ceanothus papillosus*) 129
  Ponderosa Pine (*Pinus ponderosa var. pacifica*) 129
  Bush Poppy (*Dendromecon rigida*) 130
  Yerba Santa (*Eriodictyon californicum*) 130
  Bracken Fern (*Pteridium aquilinum* var. *pubescens*) 131
  Diffuse Spineflower (*Chorizanthe diffusa*) 131
  California Rock-rose (*Helianthemum scoparium*) 132
 RIPARIAN/RIVERSIDE PLANTS 132
  Boxelder (*Acer negundo* var. *californicum*) 132
  Arroyo willow (*Salix lasiolepis*) 133
  Big Leaf Maple (*Acer macrophyllum*) 133
  Black Cottonwood (*Populus trichocarpa*) 134
  White Alder (*Alnus rhombifolia*) 134
  Western Sycamore (*Platanus racemosa*) 135
  Western Azalea (*Rhododendron occidentale*) 135
  Bleeding Hearts (*Dicentra formosa*) 136
  Dog Violet (*Viola adunca*) 136
  Giant Wake Robin (*Trillium chloropetalum*) 136
 REDWOOD AND MIXED EVERGREEN FOREST 137
  Tanoak (*Notholiyhocarpus densiflorus*) 137
  Madrone (*Arbutus menziesii*) 137
  Douglas-fir (*Pseudotsuga menziesii*) 138
  Coast Redwood (*Sequoia sempervirens*) 138
  California Bay (*Umbellularia californica*)
  (aka – Pepperwood, Bay Laurel, Bay Tree, Oregon Myrtle) 140
  Santa Cruz Mountain Oak (*Quercus parvula* var. *shrevei*) 140

    Poison Oak (*Toxicodendron diversilobum*) 141
    Swordfern (*Polystichum munitum*) 142
    California Hazelnut (*Corylus cornuta* ssp. *californica*) 142
    Western Chain Fern (*Woodwardia fimbriata*) 142
    Western Trillium (*Trillium ovatum*) 143
    California Fetid Adder's Tongue (*Scoliopus bigelovi*) 143
    Western Hound's Tongue (*Cynoglossum grande*) 144
    Milkmaids (*Cardamine californica*) 144
    Redwood Sorrel (*Oxalis oregana*) 144
  GRASSLAND/MEADOW 145
    Coyote Brush (*Baccharis pilularis* ssp. *consanguinea*) 145
    Blackberry (*Rubus ursinus*) 145
    Oats (*Avena* sp.) 146
    Beardless Wild Rye (*Elymus triticoides*) 146
    California Poppy (*Eschscholzia californica*) 147
    Common Madia (*Madia elegans*) 147
    Padre's Shooting Star (*Primula clevelandii* var. *gracillis*) 148
    Wavy Leaf Soap Plant
    (*Chlorogalum pomeridianum* var. *pomeridianum*) 148
    Purple Owl's Clover (*Castilleja exserta* ssp. *exserta*) 149
    Vetch spp. (*Vicia* spp.) 149
    Cow Parsnip (*Heracleum maximum*) 150

FAUNA **151**
  TROUT (SALMONIDAE) 151
    Coastal Rainbow Trout
    (*Oncorhynchus mykiss irideus*, aka Steelhead Trout) 151
  SALAMANDERS (CAUDATA) 152
    Rough-skinned newts (*Taricha granulosa*) 152
  SLUGS (GASTROPODA) 153
    Banana slug (*Ariolamax californicus, Ariolimax columbianus* and
    Ariolimax dolichophallus) 153
  OPOSSUMS (DIDELPHIDAE) 154
    Virginia Opossum (*Didelphis virginiana*) 154
  INSECTIVORES (INSECTIVORA) 155
    Trowbridge's Shrew (*Sorex trowbridgii*) 155
    Shrew-mole (*Neurotrichus gibbsii*) 156
    Broad-footed Mole (*Scapanus latimanus*) 157
  BATS (CHIROPTERA) 157
    Townsend's Big-eared Bat (*Corynorhinus townsendii*) 157
  HARES AND RABBITS (LAGOMORPHA) 158
    Brush Rabbit (*Sylvilagus bachmani*) 158
    Audubon's Cottontail (*Sylvilagus audubonii*) 159
    Black-tailed Jackrabbit (*Lepus californicus*) 160

RODENTS (RODENTIA) ... 160
   Merriam's Chipmunk (*Tamias merriami*) ... 160
   California Ground Squirrel (*Spermophilus beecheyi*) ... 161
   Western gray squirrel (*Sciurus griseus*) ... 161
   Botta's Pocket Gopher (*Thomomys bottae*) ... 162
      Bad Gopher Jokes. ... 163
   California Pocket Mouse (*Chaetodipus californicus*) ... 163
   Deer Mouse (*Peromyscus maniculatus*) ... 164
   Dusky-Footed Woodrat (*Neotoma fuscipes*) ... 165
   Black Rat (*Rattus rattus*) ... 166
   California Vole (*Microtus californicus*) ... 167
CARNIVORES (CARNIVORA) ... 167
   Coyote (*Canis latrans*) ... 167
   Gray Fox (*Urocyon cinereoargenteus*) ... 168
   Raccoon (*Procyon lotor*) ... 169
   Long-tailed Weasel (*Mustela frenata*) ... 170
   Striped Skunk (*Mephitis mephitis*) ... 170
      A Few Skunk Jokes (that truly stink): ... 171
   Mountain Lion (*Puma concolor*) ... 172
   Bobcat (*Felis rufus*) 173
HOOFED ANIMALS (ARTIODACTYLA) ... 174
   Mule Deer (*Odocoileus hemionus*) ... 174
NO LONGER PRESENT ... 175
   California Golden Bear, California Grizzly
   (*Ursus arctos horribilis*) ... 175
   Pronghorn (*Antilocapra var.*) ... 176

CLOSING REMARKS ... 177

ABOUT THE AUTHOR ... 178

SELECTED READING ... 179

PHOTO ATTRIBUTES ... 181

Acknowledgements

I find acknowledgements are best written after a good meal, when the heart is still and has been warmed by some moment of small contentment. I've sat with my family or with friends, we shared the pleasantries of our day and as meandering the dialogue may have been, it brought a certain ray of satisfaction to the soul. There have been a couple of times I've written my acknowledgements under the cover of a small humble glass of house red. Not today, mind you, today it was the meal that inspired me to complete this section, but that elixir of grape has its own pleasant way of loosening the spirit and allowing words to flow. Acknowledgements are my favorite part of the book, not so much to read them, but to write them. As an author, they are my moment to put my gratitude into words. You see books are not written alone. This book could not have happened but for the will and unconditional help and favor of people, many of them I met specifically and exclusively because of this book.

As the catalyst whose help started me on this journey, I want to thank Executive Director Bonny Hawley and the Friends of Santa Cruz State Parks for which she serves. She helped me create my first book, even helped create the logo for my publishing company, Gone Beyond Guides. The book, a guide for neighboring Wilder Ranch State Park was my first and without her help on that one, the book you are reading would not be in your hands.

Mountain Parks Foundation works very closely with the Friends of Santa Cruz State Parks and together they do amazing things. Both are nonprofit organizations supporting specific state parks. At both nonprofits, they work tirelessly, they are insanely dedicated, and every person on their staff goes above and beyond every day for one purpose; to better the state parks they represent. It is an altruistic and beautiful thing to witness and donating to them brings dollars that are focused directly on the represented parks.

Mountain Parks Foundation has the honor and duty to help support Henry Cowell Redwoods State Park. To them and to their Executive Director Brenda Holmes, I owe much thanks. I met Brenda about a year ago while working on the Wilder book. She was extremely helpful and this book could not have been created without her direct help. Like with Bonny, there are really no words that can fully describe the gratitude I have for both her help and for the work she does with the Mountain Parks Foundation.

On the California State Park side, I had some great moments with State Park Interpreter Daniel Williford. Daniel is a warm hearted friendly soul who gave some great tips on the park itself. Daniel also helped give excellent guidance on the flora for this book. His knowledge in Botany helped create a nice list for readers. Daniel is a huge asset to the park and to this guide book.

The California Power Works bridge photo is by permission of the John Carney and he asked that I attribute it to him and his family. He was very gracious to allow me to use that photo. John was introduced to me by Barry Brown who also helped with the history of this part of the park.

Another individual who was extremely helpful within the history section was a man by the name of Floyd D. P. Oydegaard. Floyd was well versed in Captain Isaac Graham and even gave historical talks in Santa Cruz in character years back. In my research on Graham, most of what was written had a negative slant, primarily because Graham's nature was unruly and more of that of a trapper than a man of civility. Floyd agreed with me that there was more to Graham and helped point me to resources that were less assumptive and more objective.

S.H. Cowell Foundation, for permission to use the photos of the Cowell family but also for donating the park. The S.H. Cowell Foundation works to improve the lives of children living in poverty in Northern and Central California by providing support to strengthen families and communities.

To my friend George Trager and my boys Bryce and Everest, I want to thank for accompanying me on the many hikes I took. To George especially, who I made ford the San Lorenzo in early spring more times than he wishes to remember.

A very warm thanks to Chris Henrick who created all the maps in this book. He is a master cartographer and a great person.

To the docents! I loved the docents of Henry Cowell. They know so much more than I can ever know about this wonderful park and truly care for its wellbeing and historical accuracy. They are always friendly, pleasant and extremely knowledgeable.

Finally, I want to thank Elizabeth Hammack for her efforts both within the California State Park system and in this book. For many visitors, they come to the various state parks and the park is simply there, waiting to greet them. But if you look deeper, you find a consistency to the parks. Behind the scenes are many people making this all look easy. Elizabeth is a big part of what makes the parks as great as they are today. Every visitor whose day is brightened by a visit to one of the state parks she oversees are in no small part thanks to her efforts. Few people could do what she does and make it look so effortless.

Introduction

Henry Cowell Redwoods State Park is truly one of the gems of California. Tucked off the beaten path just enough to feel like an adventure, yet still within the Bay Area, the park offers much to the visitor. For families and the casual visitor, the park offers one of the last groves of old growth coastal redwoods, the tallest trees in the world. Nearby one can take an equally peaceful walk along the often lazy San Lorenzo River. The Buckeye Trail gives a more adventurous journey, with multiple river crossings and sense of rugged remoteness.

Henry Cowell State Redwoods State Park is split into two units, the Main Unit and the Fall Creek Unit. Together, they comprise 4,650 acres with over 35 miles of hiking trails. Much of the park trails are open to mountain biking and horses with a few trails open to dogs as well. Additionally, there is seasonal camping and fishing within the park. Nearby is the privately owned Roaring Camp Railroad, which offers railroad trips and even some old west entertainment.

Most of the entire area was once owned and operated by the lime kiln tycoon Henry Cowell. Little remains of the massive operations that once occupied this area in the late 1800's to the 1940's. The echoes of the past are still evident, with ruins of both lime kilns and barrel making machinery, mainly in the Fall Creek section of the park. Plus, there is Fall Creek itself which follows faithfully alongside the visitor as they wind their way up the trail by the same name.

Besides being able to experience one of the last 3-5% of remaining old growth redwoods in the world, visitors can experience the equally unique Santa Cruz Sandhills. Created by marine sand deposited some 10 12 million years ago, this ecosystem contains 4 plants and 3 animals found nowhere else on the planet.

Whether you are looking for casual recreation along the river on a hot day, a reset of the spirit amongst the redwoods, a retrace back in time or a rewarding hike, Henry Cowell Redwoods State Park will not disappoint.

General Information

Getting There

Henry Cowell Redwoods State Park is near the town of Felton, California on or near Highway 9. The main park and the Fall Creek Unit of the park can be accessed from multiple entrance points. Directions to the main entrances are described here. For other ways to get into the park, refer to the trail descriptions and the map.

Coming from San Jose, California, take Highway 17 towards Santa Cruz. Take the Mt. Hermon Road exit and turn right. Take Mt. Hermon Road about 3.5 miles until it ends and then make a right onto Graham Hill Road. After a short 0.2 miles you will turn left on Highway 9, going through the town of Felton. The park is approximately .5 miles outside of Felton on your left.

If coming from Santa Cruz, take River Street (Highway 9) towards Felton for six miles to reach the main entrance.

The campground entrance is located off of Graham Hill Road. On reaching Graham Hill Road from Mt. Hermon Road, make a left and stay on Graham Hill for about 2.5 miles. The campgrounds will be on your right.

The Fall Creek Unit is accessed from Felton Empire Road. At the interesection of Graham Hill Road and Highway 9, simply continue straight from Graham Hill Road as it becomes Felton Grade Road for 0.6 miles.

Henry Cowell campground is located at 2591 Graham Hill Road, Scotts Valley, CA 95060. For day use, the address is 101 North Big Trees Park Road, Felton, CA 95018.

Parking

Just after the entrance toll gate there is ample parking at the main lot. Alternatively, there are several areas to park and enter the park scattered along Graham Hill Road, Felton Grade Road and Highway 9. Parking in the main lot is $10 and is typically safe from theft, whereas parking off the roads and highways are free, albeit at your own risk.

There is also a parking lot for the Fall Creek Unit on the right hand side of Felton Grade Road just past Ley Road shortly after leaving the town of Felton.

For descriptions on the additional parking to be had, refer to the corresponding trail heads in the Trails Section.

Gas, Food, Lodging

There are plenty of places to get gas, dine and stay overnight within the towns of nearby Felton and Scotts Valley. Both are smaller towns and as they are somewhat isolated from the main stream sectors of the Bay Area, you may find that prices are slightly higher. Both towns aren't too small however and as they are isolated, the services within these towns are complete and whole. One may not find the large mega stores found in the greater Bay Area and even Santa Cruz, but you will be able to find multiple choices for everything you need.

During the many trips to Henry Cowell, I would hit Salsa's Taco Bar in Scott's Valley. This clean well lit place has a good salsa bar selection, decent chips, cold drinks and huge portions, which are well received after a long hike. Being able to jump right onto Highway 17 afterwards was another plus.

Operating Hours, Amenities and Telephone

The day use areas of the park are open daily from sunrise to sunset. Overnight camping is also permitted.

The park has a very nice visitor c enter that is open daily from 10am to 4pm, staff permitting. In the winter the Center is open from 11am to 3pm during the weekdays.

The Nature Store opens each day at 10am, with different seasonal closing times.

Amenities include restrooms, a bookstore, the above mentioned Visitor Center and Nature Store as well as guided tours, exhibits, historic sites and family programs given by the rangers. There are some snack food items as well as local books in the Nature Store. Picnic tables are available near the parking area and other areas as shown on the map.

Other telephone numbers:

Day Use Kiosk: 831-335-4598

Visitor Center: 831-335-7077

Nature Store: 831-335-3174

Camping

Camping is allowed in the park at the Henry Cowell campground located off of Graham Hill Road. There is no camping allowed at the Fall Creek Unit. Camping is $35 per night for vehicles. The fee will allow one vehicle and one towed vehicle entry. This is a Hike and Bike friendly park, so if you are coming via bike or foot, the fee is just $7 per person. An individual can camp at Henry Cowell for up to 30 days in any calendar year. The campgrounds are open from May 1 to October 30th typically and are closed in the winter.

Max Camper Length: 35 Feet

Max Trailer Length: 31 Feet

The campgrounds have full restrooms, fire rings, showers, phone and wood available for purchase from the campground host. Some campsites are ADA compliant.

There are restrictions on minors camping in the park. Persons under the age of 15-18 who are not camping with a parent or legal guardian must obtain written permission to camp in the park. Children 14 years of age and under must be accompanied by a parent or legal guardian. Contact the park for details regarding camping as a minor.

The perfect campground spot is a matter of personal choice. Many of the spots in the Henry Cowell Campground get good marks for overall privacy, ability to accommodate either a tent or RV and flatness of terrain. There are a few that standout within these qualities and are listed below.

Campsites 74 – 84 sit on or near the canyon's edge and offer a view across the park with 74-76 being the standouts in this category. On the flip side, Campsites 86-113 were noted for being "okay" on the privacy score. This score is not horrible, it just means the sites are either near a restroom or in sight of other campers. As far as the terrain goes, Campsites 92-113 were all rated as flat terrain along with campsites 23-35.

Reservations can be made online via Reserve America at www.reserveamerica.com. The site also has a full list of rules, fees and other details not listed here. You can also reserve by calling the park at 800-444-7275.

The campground address is: 2591 Graham Hill Road, Scotts Valley, CA 95060. The campground kiosk phone is 831-438-2396

Fees

Day use fees are $10 and as shown below. Camping fees detailed in camping section. Fees are subject to change.

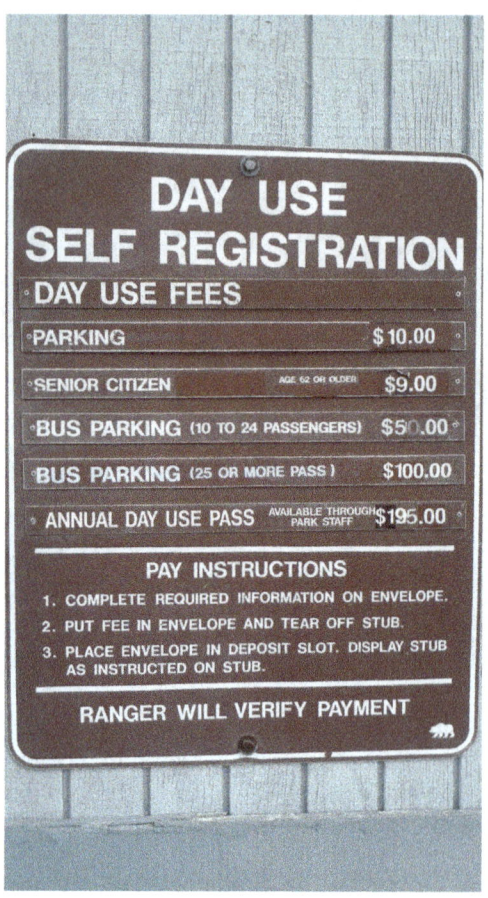

Handicap Accessibility

Henry Cowell contains five campground sites that are designated accessible. These sites contain accessible tables and fire rings. The restroom near campsite #22 is generally accessible as are the toilets and showers. All routes to restrooms are generally accessible within the campground.

The Visitor Center and most of the exhibits within are generally accessible. The route from the parking area to the Visitor Center is 350 feet and is accessible, though there is a slight threshold that may require some assistance. For those with mobility issues, please call the Visitor Center.

There are three trails that are partially accessible. The Redwood Loop Interpretative Trail near the Visitor Center is accessible for approximately 0.7 miles. There is an audio version of the interpretive stops within the trail that can be downloaded for free via this link: http://www.parks.ca.gov/?page_id=27184.

The other two trails that have some accessibility are the Meadow Trail and River Trail. The Meadow Trail is accessible for about 0.50 miles starting at the trailhead. The River Trail, in the same area is accessible for the first 4,000 feet. Access starts off the Meadow Trail about 0.2 miles in from the trailhead.

Dogs, Horses, Hikers and Mountain Bikes

With the exception of service animals, dogs are allowed in a limited fashion within the park. Visitors can bring their dogs to the picnic areas and along the Pipeline Road, Graham Hill Trail, Power Mill Fire Road and Meadow Trail. Dogs are only allowed on these trails. Dogs must be on leash no longer than six feet at all times. Dogs are not allowed on the Redwood Loop Trail.

Dogs are also allowed in the campground but must be kept inside your car or tent at night.

There are ample opportunities for the equestrian at Henry Cowell. Horses are allowed within the Henry Cowell and Fall Creek Unit with the exception of the Ox Trail, Pipeline Road south of Rincon Fire Road, Meadow Trail and Redwood Grove Trail. Horse trailers are allowed at the Powder Mill Trail Head. There are two staging areas, one at Henry Cowell at the main entrance and one at the Bennett Creek Trailhead at Fall Creek. There are additional restrictions to a few trails within Fall Creek. Refer to the trail markers themselves for details.

Mountain biking is prohibited in the Fall Creek Unit as well as all hiking trails with the exception of Pipeline Road, Rincon Fire Road, Ridge Fire Road, and Powder Mill Fire Road. Cyclists may be cited, especially between the UC Santa Cruz/Henry Cowell borders to Highway 9. That being said, mountain bikers do love Henry Cowell, so keep a watchful eye out, especially if travelling on any of the steeper trails where the biker can really pick up speed. We had one incident on Lost Empire Trail where the group coming down was travelling so fast that the lead biker had to lay down his bike to avoid hitting us. Fortunately, no one was hurt.

Hikers are allowed on all trails.

Weather by Season and Recommended Clothing

Henry Cowell Redwoods State Park is typically warm to hot in the summer and mild but rainy during the winter season. The Santa Cruz Mountains in general catch much of the rain that comes in from the Pacific Ocean. The nearby town of Felton receives an average of 49.1 inches of rain per year. Summer highs can be in the mid-eighties and winter lows just above freezing, on average.

Within Henry Cowell Redwoods State Park, the best options for clothing are to bring interchangeable layers. Another consideration, especially in summer is the drastic difference in climate between the Bay Area and the Coast. The Bay Area may be hot and dry, leaving the traveler to decide on T-shirt and shorts as the clothing of choice. It's only when you get over the hill and see the coastal marine layer of fog that you realize you should have brought something warmer to wear. Best advice is to bring the sweatshirt and windbreaker; you can always leave them in the car if they aren't needed.

What to Do, See and Know

Henry Cowell Redwoods State Park is made up of two sections, the main Henry Cowell Redwoods State Park and the nearby Fall Creek Unit.

Fall Creek offers a little less than 20 miles of hiking trails over 2,390 acres. The trails are designed for hiking and equestrian travel. Within the Fall Creek Unit it's easy to get a feeling of remoteness fast that increases the deeper into the park you travel. Within the forest are some great examples of old growth redwood trees, some of which could be between 1400 to 1800 years of age. This unit also contains a fairly well preserved example of lime kilns.

Henry Cowell Main Unit offers a wide variety of activities for the visitor. There are 15 miles of hiking and equestrian trails with a few trails being dog friendly. Visitors can also camp during the summer months and engage in catch and release fishing for steelhead during the winter months.

Henry Cowell has a great Visitor Center and bookstore. Close to parking and the Visitor Center, the Redwood Grove Loop Trail offers an easy trip into old growth redwoods, some of which is handicap accessible. Also nearby is the neighboring Roaring Camp Railroad. While not operated by the park, access from the park is straightforward. Roaring Camp Railroads offer "trips back in time" on old steam engine trains over various routes within the Santa Cruz Mountains. They also hold a number of special events throughout the year, many in conjunction with major holidays.

Park History

Native People

Prior to American settlers, the Spanish, Mexican and even Russian cultures, there was the Ohlone culture. The Ohlone lived in what is commonly referred to today as the Bay Area, extending from San Francisco down to Big Sur. They fished, hunted, harvested, married, traded and were a sophisticated group relative to their peers. They had a high degree of ornamentation in dress and custom as well as rich soulful ceremonial practices. They held in a deep and complex spiritual foundation, with its own creation myths, accords on living with each other and with the land in which they lived. They believed in the existence of spirit animals and had their own notion of what happens to a person in the afterlife. Within the Bay Region, there were some 40-50 different communities, each with its own leader, territory and often very unique sub cultures.

Archeological dating puts the Ohlone people in the Bay Area from as early as 4000 BC by some accounts and even as far back as the Ice Age 10-16,000 years ago. They are considered to be a very ancient culture, surpassing even the Plains Indians. They held a strong spiritual bond with the land and with each other. The Ohlone are known for their active management of the land and they learned to perform controlled burns and other techniques to increase production of game and harvestable plants. As a result, when the Spanish arrived in 1769, they were met with an abundance of wild life, which was due in large part to their active management of the natural resources. Grizzly bears, elk and pronghorn, salmon, perch and a plentitude of various waterfowl roamed the land amongst massive stands of old growth redwoods and other trees. Along the oceans, sea lions were in such vast quantity that they "looked like pavement", according to early Majorcan missionary and European explorer, Juan Crespi.

The community that occupied the area from Davenport to Aptos along the coast was made up of the Awaswas language group. Further inland within the boundaries of Henry Cowell were the Zayante language group. Along the coast the Ohlone made tule boats from the extensive wetlands in the area (most of which are gone today) to fish and gather marine fowl and mammals. The Ohlone enjoyed a rich abundance of wildlife and for the almost 6000 years they inhabited the region, they were able to exist as hunter gatherers, never needing to learn how to farm. Even when settlers came to the region, the abundance of fowl in the wetlands was so extensive that "when alarmed by a rifle shot they would rise in a dense cloud with a noise like that of a hurricane".

Trading was a huge component of the culture and the Ohlone had one of the most valuable of the traded items, sea shells. Many were chiseled, polished and even cut to add to their value. Shells were highly tradable items further inland, becoming to tribes that had never even seen the ocean something of an almost mythical quality. For example, the Shoshone of the Mojave Desert were known to highly revere shells as part of their religious ceremonies.

When the Spanish arrived in 1769, there were between 10,000 -26,000 Ohlone's living in the Bay Area. Their stability and complex infrastructure was interrupted with disastrous results for the people. The mission of Santa Cruz was one of seven missions built under the direction of Junipero Serra with the objective of establishing a chain of missions to populate the territories to create a tax base by converting the Ohlone and other native peoples to Christianity. The missions acted to disrupt the social structure and overall Ohlone culture. Many of the Ohlone were moved to the missions where they faced overcrowding and then subsequent disease, infant mortality and miscarriages that led to a spiral of brutal demise for the people. In one incident in the spring of 1806, the native culture lost over one quarter of their population to a measles outbreak.

By 1834 the Mexican government secularized the missions and the Ohlone people. While now in a less controlled state, they watched as their land was divided again into vast Mexican owned ranchos. By this time, it is estimated that the Ohlone population was a mere 10 percent of what it was prior to the Spanish arrival. The remaining Ohlone men became the ranch hands and cowboys that worked the land owned by the Rancho owners. When the Gold Rush came in 1848, the California population boomed, bringing a new wave of disease that pushed the Ohlone population further into decline and near extinction. The Ohlone were custodians of a wilder, more abundant California for over 6,000 years. They lived in harmony with the land and with each other. After all that time, in just 58 years their culture was changed forever.

As sober and heartbreaking as this story is, the Ohlone still survive today. As of 2005 there are at least 1400 Ohlone living in scattered small communities throughout the Bay Area. For the most part they continue to practice and retain many of the beliefs and ceremonial structures that had served them prior to the Spanish, Mexican and American occupation.

The Mexican Ranchos

The occupation and missionaries of the Spanish changed in 1821 when Mexico gained independence from Spain. With growing insurgence, the Mexican people engaged in ten years of civil war to acquire their independence from the Spanish. California, which was seen as a high water mark in the Spanish conquests also proved to be a costly venture for the Spanish to maintain and as part of the agreement, ownership of "Alta California" was transferred to the Mexican Government. The City of Monterey was made the state capital of Mexico's new state which they named Alta California.

During this time, the Mexican Governors of Alta California allowed for individuals to own California land. By 1824, these codes for granting land were firmly established. Land grants increased in 1833, when the new government ordered the secularization (decommissioning) of the Spanish missions. All of the vast lands surrounding the mission ranchos were repossessed, leaving the mission padres with only the church, the priest's quarters and the humble priest's garden.

It was at this point that three ranchos came into the picture, three ranchos that together covered the current boundaries of Henry Cowell Redwoods State Park. These three were the Rancho Carbonera, Rancho Zayante and the Rancho Cañada del Rincon en el Rio San Lorenzo. Each of these ranchos (and many like them) met the same fate. They would each be granted to a Californio or Yankee Pioneer who became a Mexican Citizen. Then the United States went to war with the Mexican Government, the war lasted eighteen months, the US won and all land ownership had to now be proven under US law. A few Mexican landowners found themselves lucky and had a defensible copy of their land deed. Most though fought costly and lengthy legal battles that resulted in their complete loss of ownership rights.

Rancho Carbonera

The northern portion of the 2,225-acre (9.00km2) Rancho Carbonera encompasses the southern portion of the current Henry Cowell Redwoods State Park. The Rancho extended further south towards Santa Cruz and includes the current Pasatiempo Golf Course. It was designated as lying between the San Lorenzo River and Branciforte Creek. The Rancho Carbonera's first landowner was Captain William Buckle.

William Buckle was an English sea captain of the whaling vessel Daniel IV. While by their own admission that William came to California with his brother Samuel in 1823, there are other documented newspaper articles surrounding an incident of slavery in Hawaii in 1826. This conflict put Buckle's own claim in question. While William's main tie to Henry Cowell Redwoods State Park is through his grant of Rancho Carbonera, the event in Hawaii is worth a short pause and gives some insight on William Buckle himself.

The story begins in Lahaina Hawaii where the Reverends William Richards and Charles Stewart along with their wives made an arduous decision to build a school and take on missionary studies with the locals beginning in April, 1823. They learned the Hawaiian language and then taught the locals about the gospel in their native tongue. Reverend Richards became the voice of the mission to the English press through his letters sent with ships coming in from Hawaii to newspapers in England.

One account by Richards that became a joint formal outcry from a number of missionaries was published in New England's Missionary Herald regarding a port of call by Captain William Buckle into Lahaina in 1825. The article was titled, "Outrage of a Whale-ship's Crew" and in effect stated that Captain Buckle had purchased a Hawaiian girl as his slave for 10 dubloons, about $160 at the time. The Reverend stated that the girl, herself an important Hawaiian Chief named Leoiki, went against her will. The article describes a scene where she repeatedly requests help to get her off the ship that ultimately leads to an armed standoff between the locals and the missionaries on one side and Buckle's crew on the other.

The account of piracy against William Buckle had gone untested for over 180 years until a descendent of both Captain Buckle and Leoiki presented a rebuttal against these claims in a paper given in 2008 at the Annual Symposium on Maritime Archeology and History of Hawaii. The descendent, Isaaca Hanson refutes the claim, saying that Captain Buckle actually brought Leoiki on board to marry her and that the two bore a son together. Chief Leoiki was a high ranking member of the Royal Hawaiian family and would have been unlikely that she would be allowed to be sold off to a whaling captain for any amount of money. Perhaps the most supportive evidence towards William Buckle's innocence was that he was never charged with piracy. Slavery was abolished in England in 1807 and was punishable by death at that time.

The Daniel IV ultimately sunk off of Tahiti carrying oil that leaked and caught on fire. William Buckle retired as a Captain upon coming to California with his brother Samuel and set out to get a land grant from Mexico. The process for obtaining land grants required the grantee to become a naturalized citizen, learn to speak Spanish, marry into the Mexican bloodlines, and change both his religion and his name. Thus William Buckle became Jose Guillermo Bocle and marry into the reputable Castro family by marrying Maria Antonia Castro. He was granted the Rancho Carbonera by Govenor Alvarado in 1838.

William Buckle had many aliases beyond Jose Guillermo. He was also known as Boc, Bucle, Bocle, Mead and both he and his brother later changed their last names to Thompson. There isn't any recorded reason for the name changes, though it is recorded that William took a considerable hit to his reputation due to the event in Hawaii.

William built what is believed to be the first paper mill in California on his land along the San Lorenzo River in 1860. The mill in some ways was also one of the first to recycle waste products. The logging of the surrounding redwood forests produced an abundance of pulp. The mill used the water from the San Lorenzo River to turn the pulp into course brown wrapping paper, producing a ton of the product daily. The paper was loaded onto ships in nearby Santa Cruz and distributed to the fast growing city of San Francisco. That being said, the mill only lasted two years. Two disasters would soon befall the plant from which it would never recover. The winter storms of 1861/62 destroyed portions of the mill but even more devastating, the managing superintendent Henry Van Valkenburg was killed by a falling tree. He left behind his wife Ellen and their three children and she actually tried to run the mill herself for a short period. In the end, the mill was auctioned off and sold to the California Powder Works for $20,026.

Rancho Zayante

Rancho Zayante was a Mexican land grant comprising 2,656 acres (10.76 km2) and straddled its namesake Zayante Creek and the San Lorenzo River. This area included most of present day Felton, Mount Hermon, Olympia and parts of Ben Lomond and Quail Hollow. The grant was first given to a San Jose teacher named Joaquin Buelna in 1834. Not much is known of Joaquin other than he was one of the Acalde's (municipal magistrate) of Branciforte, which is now a part of Santa Cruz. It is also known that he never occupied the land and since the owner had to build a home on the granted land within the first year, his grant lapsed and the entire Rancho was re-granted to Joseph Ladd Majors in 1841.

Majors was a fur trapper from Tennessee who came over with Isaac Graham in 1834 and was one of the few Californian's to make it to the state before the Gold Rush. To obtain land he followed the rules by becoming a Mexican citizen and temporarily changed his name to Juan Jose Crisostomo Mayor. In 1839 Joseph married one of the three daughters of Don Jose Joaquin Castro, one of the original Mexican land Dons, who owned Rancho San Andres further south along the Monterey Bay.

With the marriage to Maria de Los Angeles, John Majors acquired Rancho Zayante. While Major's name was officially on the deed, he immediately sold the Rancho to his friend Isaac Graham. See the section on Isaac Graham for further details on this.

The three daughters of Don Jose owned land themselves. Maria, Maria de Los Angeles, and Jacinta Antonia were granted the Rancho Refugio that is now known as Wilder Ranch State Park. Since Joseph had married Maria de Los Angeles, he and his wife held title not only to the Rancho Zayante but also to a third of Rancho Refugio. While the three sisters owned Rancho Refugio, the husband of the other Maria, a Russian otter fur trader named Osip Volkov (aka José Antonio Bolcoff), rewrote the Rancho Refugio deed in his own name, cutting off any claim Majors and his wife had to the property. (See my book, The Complete Guide to Wilder Ranch State Park for a full write up of Bolcoff and his contributions to the area).

Joseph Majors and Maria de Los Angeles had 22 children, 19 of which lived to adulthood. Joseph and Isaac Graham stayed close as informal business and political partners. Both were part of a growing population of Yankees that were seeking their own prosperity amongst the Spanish speaking Californios. While unrest in Texas between the Yankees and Mexicans was making most of the headlines at this time, there was an equal amount of unrest mounting in Alta California. The tension came to a head in 1840 when a party led by Graham and including Joseph Majors and 44 other English and Yankee frontiersman were arrested for treason. Joseph's wife Maria de Los Angeles successfully petitioned for the release of her husband. Graham and his party were shipped to San Blas Mexico and become part of a multinational crisis known as the "Graham Affair". (See Captain Isaac Graham).

Majors enjoyed a tremendous advantage as a naturalized Mexican citizen. Prior to California's inclusion into the United States, Majors acquired land in his name and then sold or leased the land to his Yankee counterparts. The first power sawmill in California was built on the Rancho Zayante near the current town of Felton which Majors gave the rights to in 1841. At Rancho San Augustin Majors built the first secular flour mill and tanneries in the state. In 1843 Majors built a grist mill along Laurel Creek. The mill was quite an attraction, costing $12,000 to build and was an important operation for the surrounding communities.

Farmers came as far as Santa Clara, loading up their wheat grains onto the backs of burros and making the long trek over the trails of the Santa Cruz Mountains to have their wheat ground into flour. A portion of the flour was received by the mill as payment.

Majors became the first mayor of Santa Cruz during the very short lived Bear Flag Republic and when the State was officially admitted to the Union he was elected to represent the city at the state's first constitutional convention held in Monterey. He was also the first treasurer of Santa Cruz County and when given the first tax funds he placed it in the safest place he could find, which was under the bed of his friend Moses Meder!

Between 1848 and 1852, the former Alta California underwent dramatic changes. It was now part of the United States and no longer under Mexican rule, but even more dramatic, its population exploded from an estimated 15,000 residents to over 300,000. All claims to land had to be proven by the United States. During this time many of the Mexican Don's either lost control of their land outright or through expensive and long legal battles. For Majors, his claim to Rancho Zayante officially went to Isaac Graham, who he had held the land for, however his claim for rights to a third of Rancho Refugio was not recognized. Remember that José Antonio Bolcoff had rewritten the deed in his own name, cutting out the three daughters that actually owned the land. Jose Bolcoff's deed was recognized as the legitimate one and Joseph Major and his wife, one of the three daughters, lost claim to the land.

In a twist of fate, Jose Bolcoff himself lost the rights to another Rancho he owned, the Rancho San Agustin (pronounced a-goo-stin). He couldn't prove he owned the land under the eyes of the United States government and the person who first filed claim to it was none other than Joseph Majors. In 1852 Majors sold Rancho San Agustin to a young seaman from Maine by the name of Hiram Scott. Hiram came for gold like many at the time but unlike the many that came, Hiram actually struck it big in the gold fields and later added to his wealth through a ferry business in Stockton. He traveled to the Santa Cruz area and purchased the area that is today known as Scott's Valley.

There is an interesting side note between the Scott family and another famous historical family, the Bennetts. The Bennett-Arcane parties were the members of the original prospector families that became stranded in a dry scorching god forsaken land that upon finally leaving they dubbed "Death Valley". The Bennett family finally settled in Watsonville, the Arcane family in Santa Cruz. When Mr. Bennett's wife Sarah died, husband Asa Bennett could not take care of their newborn baby Ella and gave it to the Scott's to raise as their own. William Manly, the member of the party that both rescued the Bennett Arcane party and wrote one of the finest historical accounts on the ordeal in Death Valley would one day visit Ella when she was fully grown.

Going back to John Majors, while he prospered in the 1850's, a severe drought in 1863-1864 nearly bankrupted the family. John died a poor man in 1868. In 1879 their family home burned down and Maria de Los Angeles, the once proud and rich daughter of one of the wealthiest families in Mexico would eventually have all of her land and wealth stripped from her by lawyers who fought on her behalf with land as payment. Still she was respected in the area, primarily for her skills as an herbalist. Late in life she gave her views on the transgressions she endured in an interview in Santa Cruz Sentinel:

"Years ago, thousands of acres of land were mine, and horses and cattle and sheep enough to keep sheep herders busy from rise to set of sun. Then I had fine houses and chests of money and silk dresses and laces and jewelry and friends, ah!, many friends…But the beautiful house on the hill was burned. My husband died, my boys drank the wine and played the cards, and the Americanos came like hungry wolves…

"Today I am old and poor. The young lawyers who were my friends and who made the papers for me are all very rich…They have hundreds of acres of land and much money, while I sit here like an old owl in a dark corner and tell those who ask me that these men have robbed me of all that was mine by their crooked talk and their crooked laws."

Rancho Cañada del Rincon en el Rio San Lorenzo

Nicknamed Rancho Rincon, this 5,827-acre (23.58km2), the full name of the rancho means the "valley on a corner on the San Lorenzo River". The grant sat north of Santa Cruz on the San Lorenzo River. The grant was originally given to a Frenchman by the name of Pedro Sainsevain.

At the age of 21 Pedro was sent from his hometown of Bordeaux, France to find his uncle Jean-Louis Vignes in Los Angeles. He arrived in Santa Barbara in 1839, found his uncle and began helping grow grapes and oranges on the uncle's property. The Frenchmen brought their craft of winemaking to the area and in 1840, Pedro sailed some of his wine and brandy up the California coast for sale. It was during this trip he made his first visit to Monterey and Branciforte.

Pedro actually received the land grant of two leagues prior to his becoming a Mexican citizen, a requirement under law. He operated one of the first sawmills along the San Lorenzo River as well as a flour mill along the Guadalupe River in San Jose. By 1845 he married Paula Suñol a daughter of nearby rancho owner Antonio Suñol.

The flour mill was operated with his partner Charles Roussillon, another Frenchman. The two built a schooner together that they named the Antonita on the beach of Santa Cruz. They sailed it to Hawaii, then called the Sandwich Islands. Charles by the way was sued by Isaac Graham in 1847 for "shipping his wood away". Don Pedro was asked to be a defendant to what was actually the first jury trial in California. (Charles was acquitted of any fraudulent intent, though the jury did award $65 to the "American whom nobody liked").

Don Pedro and Charles tried their luck as one of the first Gold Rush miners, mining at Don Pedro's Bar on the Toulumne River in 1848. Like many of these Gold Rush stories, they tried and returned without much to show for their efforts. Not to be defeated, they both opened up a miners supply store in Stockton and made more money in that venture. By the way, if "Don Pedro" sounds familiar, his gold mining days did bring him two namesake legacies, the Don Pedro Reservoir and Don Pedro Dam.

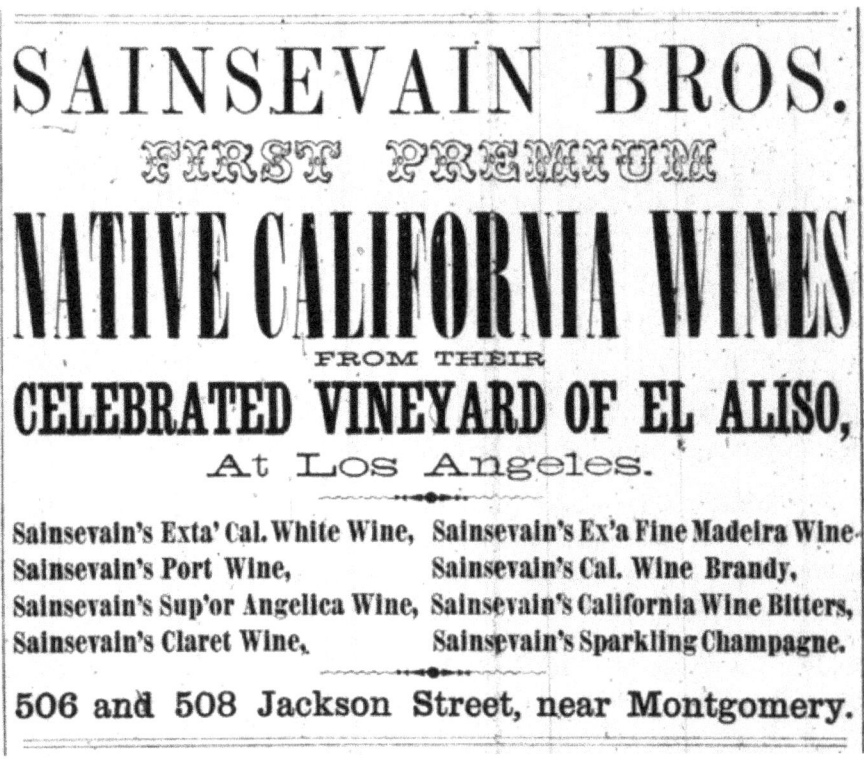

In 1859, Don Pedro traded his Rancho with the Davis and Jordan Lime Company for a rather large coastal steamer dubbed the "Santa Cruz". Don Pedro tried a run with the steamer but finally sold it to new owners (who somehow got it to the Yangtse River where it burned down in 1861). With the ship's proceeds he bought his uncle's vineyards the El Aliso down in Los Angeles where life had started for him as a young man. He tried to expand the vineyard's operations with the help of his brother Jean Louis and is considered the first producer of sparkling wine in California, but aside from some small successes at county fairs, the wine venture ran dry.

In the year of his wife's death in 1883, Pierre Don Pedro Sainsevain; French Settler, Mexican, American and notable historical figure of California, returned to France where he lived until his death on October 4th, 1904.

California Powder Works

The California Powder Works was the first explosive powder manufacturing company not only in California but west of the Rockies. Incorporated in 1861, it began manufacturing gunpowder in May, 1864. The company was an impressive operation and a major employer for Santa Cruz County, employing between 150 and 275 men. It operated for 50 years on what was originally the Rancho Carbonera. The plant closed in 1914.

The California Powder Works was established as a result of a directive given during the Civil War. Shipments of all gunpowder from the East Coast to California were halted during the war for fear that it would fall into the hands of the Confederates. That presented a problem as the Industrial Revolution was in full gear in California and the West. Railroads were expanding at a rapid rate, as was construction and mining. There was money to be made but all required gunpowder to help pave and carve this expansion forward.

With that, California Powder Works became an important supplier of dynamite and gunpowder for the western expansion. In fact, the company is listed as one of the key suppliers in the creation of the Trans Continental Railroad. The plant developed new refinements that increased the gunpowder consistency and accuracy to the point that they were granted a license to produce artillery grade powder for the US Navy. Between 1892 and 1897 the Navy provided a number of cannons to use to prove out their gunpowder batches. The largest was an 8 inch diameter 32 caliber cannon that occasionally misfired and on two occasions ended up landing as far away as Felton.

The powder mill was originally powered by water from the San Lorenzo River. From the site of the Diversion Dam Trail the water actually went 1200 feet through a manmade tunnel cut into the mountain to a series of flumes that carried the water to the plant. The tunnel has since collapsed and the flumes were torn down when electricity was brought in to replace the water power. Remnants of both the dam and the flumes can still be seen.

Misfiring cannons were the least of the operation's problems. The company instilled very strict rules to minimize accidents, including prohibiting wearing shoes with metal in the soles. Despite the safety precautions, the plant experienced numerous explosions. In some cases no one would be hurt and the mill portion that was blown up was rebuilt in a week. In a couple of cases, workers were killed; one notable death was of a native of Ireland named William Manseau. William had worked at the mill since he was a boy and his father was one of the pioneer powder makers. At 40 years of age he met his fate when the Press Mill exploded throwing him out of the building. He left behind his wife and seven children.

It was in 1898 that the California Powder Works, the largest and most important gunpowder producer in the west, was rocked by a series of three consecutive explosions. Late in the afternoon at 5:15 PM, a series of explosions killed thirteen men and boys. The blasts completely blew out all of the windows of the nearby Peyton mansions belonging to the Powder Work's Superintendent. Flying glass narrowly missed the superintendent's wife.

The Santa Cruz Sentinel reported on April 27, 1898:

"At 5:15 P.M. Tuesday this city was startled by three explosions following each other in rapid succession. The heavy smoke that hung over the Powder Works told too well where the explosions had taken place. Soon Pacific Avenue was crowded with people whose faces bore anxious looks, for many had relatives and friends employed at the mills. Soon every available vehicle was on its way to the scene. When the Sentinel reporter reached a point within a half mile of Powder Mill Flat another explosion occurred."

Fires broke out and rescuers worked at a frantic pace throughout the night to keep the fires from moving to the more southern powder magazines. It took over a week to find the remains and identify the victims. One was never found. In the end, thirteen men and boys were killed and another twenty five were injured. It was by far the deadliest disaster the mill would encounter.

Thirty years prior to "The Great Explosion of 1898", east coast based Dupont purchased what would eventually become a 43% interest in the California Powder Works. By 1903 Dupont took full interest in the mill and the other mills the Powder Works operated. In 1912, Dupont became the target of an antitrust lawsuit becoming so large it was required to split into three separate firms. By 1914, the plant's operations in Santa Cruz were terminated.

There is one more side note of fame that can be attributed to the California Powder Works. They brand name for their blasting powder was Hercules Powder after the Greek demigod of strength. As the California Powder Works expanded operations, it moved its nitroglycerin manufacturing facility to a relatively isolated location near the San Pablo Bay. They set up company housing and named the town Hercules, which continues to thrive today.

Captain Isaac Graham

It has been written that for long periods in his life, Isaac Graham spent more time with his horse then he did people. This helps in understanding the man, for at his roots he was a frontiersman, a man who preferred living deep in the untamed wilderness. He was at home fording rivers in search of game in the summer and when the snows of winter came, he was content in building a makeshift shelter in a quiet valley and staying put until the ground thawed enough to allow him to roam again.

He came to Alta California under Mexican rule and yet would never abide by the rules they set. His rebellion made him a central figure of an international crisis, one that was by some accounts the beginning of the end of Mexican rule over California. He underwent horrific torture, both fighting Indians as enemies and alongside them as friends. He sat on the Santa Cruz Council and built the first water powered sawmill in California's. Isaac even brought the mill's reputation as a "Wild and Roaring Camp" by serving up homemade whiskey. The story of Isaac Graham is one that is a part of California history, a story of a true pioneer, a man of grit and even principle, though his principles would often put him at odds with those around him.

Birth, Early Days as a Trapper

Isaac Graham was born on September 1, 1800 in Fincastle County, Virginia. The state had been admitted into the Union just 12 years prior. His love for hunting and horses started at a young age and he was known as an excellent shot. He travelled for two years with the famous explorer, trapper and politician Daniel Boone. When Daniel Boone died in 1820, Isaac was amongst the friends at his bedside.

Graham settled down briefly in Kentucky long enough to marry Miss Elizabeth Jones and have two sons and two daughters. During this time he became a full time trapper, spending the next three years with a very young Kit Carson trapping pelts. Married life never sat well with Isaac, as neither his first marriage to Miss Jones nor another marriage later in life would end on good terms. On his first marriage Isaac claimed that they were attacked and killed by Indians, but in reality Mrs. Graham took the kids and moved them to Texas.

The year after his wife left he joined a group of some 40 men, one of which was Joseph Majors. Together the group traveled together towards Alta California, then a vast territory under Mexican rule and encompassing the whole of present day California, Arizona, Nevada, Utah and even parts of Colorado and Wyoming.

Indian Attack in the Rockies

Isaac as a young man was of a massive frame, clothed in buckskin shirt and buckskin pants, a rifle over his shoulder and a well-worn wide brimmed hat

covering his unkempt hair and beard. He took a full three years trapping his way across North America before finally entering into California. During this time, he mainly lived off the land, hunting for food and trapping beaver pelts during the warmer seasons. He was attacked by various Indian tribes along the way, saw friends killed and horses stolen. In one account in the Rocky Mountains four miles from their camp, Isaac and a hunting companion by the name of George Nidever were hunting buffalo when his buddy spotted an Arapaho Indian watching them. The two men took off running and according to George they found themselves running away from a group of about 80 Indians in total. About a mile in the distance was a patch of trees that could give them cover so that's where they ran. Said his friend George:

"Graham was a good runner, in fact, the best in the party. Had he wished, he could have soon left me in the rear, but it was not his character to desert a comrade in danger, so we kept together, straining every nerve to reach the shelter of the woods. The Indians on horseback gained on us at once, and we were obliged to turn alternately, and by aiming at them, check them for the moment. Under any other circumstances, it would have been amusing to see them make their horses jump quickly from side to side. We soon realized that each stoppage was enabling those on foot to press forward."

What happened next was a surprise. The Indians were very close and capture was eminent and yet the Indians threw down their weapons as they swooped in. Nidever saw this and prevented Graham from taking fire at them. The Arapahos took hold of their captives, forced them to sit on the ground and formed a circle around the two men. In time, Graham and Nidever learned the Indians wanted to take them back to their camp, which they did.

The Arapahos actually camped alongside the trappers that evening. During the night the Pawnee Indian tribe came to the camp and a battle broke out with the Arapaho actually siding with the trappers. In the end, several horses were killed in the scuttle and some of the trappers were wounded, but none killed.

Graham First Arrives in California

Isaac Graham found his way to Monterey, California in 1833 or 1834 depending on the account related. Alta California had been under Mexican rule for twelve years at this point with Monterey as its capital. Mexicans immigrating to California were called Californios while those coming from the east were Yankees. The Californios imposed their own taxes and rules for owning land. To own land one had to become a naturalized citizen of Mexico even to the point of changing their name and religion. Many, like Isaac's friend Joseph Majors did just that, changing his name to Juan Jose Crisostomo Mayor and acquiring thousands of acres of land in the process.

Isaac on the other hand seemed to flaunt the established rules. He set up a distillery and saloon in a tule hut near Monterey, in addition to raising horses and cattle. The saloon attracted many, particularly the salt of the earth folk that were like Isaac, frontiersman who had roamed from the wilderness back east until it stopped at the shores of the Pacific. These men would come in handy for a revolution with Isaac as their leader. A certain group of Californios provided the momentum.

In 1836, the Texas Yankees were defining their own lines with Mexico, which not only put a strain on the Mexican army but raised questions amongst both the Yankees and Californios out west. The Californios were the loudest voice and several, including Vallejo, Alvarado, Castro, Pico and the Carillo brothers, wanted to secede from Mexico and become a self-ruled independent country. Still, their voice wasn't truly unified as Californios farther south had their own opinions on what self-rule meant and even where the capital should sit.

There is one more figure to bring in to begin to tell what happened next. At this point we have Isaac Graham and his surly friends. We have the outspoken Californios intent on a rebellion, with Juan Bautista Alvarado and Jose Castro being the main players for this story. The final figure is Nicholas Guiterrez, the Governor of the Alta California territories. Nicholas imposed a new levy of taxes handed down by the main land of Mexico, which ignited the rebellion.

Alvarado decided to take matters into his own hands and went to Isaac, saying that if he and his men helped Alvarado, he promised Graham and his men large tracts of land, citizenship and equal rights to all Yankees. He also stated that if Graham didn't help, the Yankees would be arrested and exiled. Graham should have seen this counter proposal as a warning of Alvarado's true allegiance, but instead he accepted Alvarado's call to arms saying, "I will call around me here a force that will make the old devil of a Mexican tremble."

Graham named the 50 men he had gathered for the fight the "Rifleros Americanos". Together with Alvarado's troops they marched to the governor's mansion in Monterey. Alvarado first surrounded the mansion and ordered for Governor Nicholas Guiterrez to surrender. Despite the Governor's own men deserting their posts, Nicholas refused to give in. For two days Alvarado tried to gain control without bloodshed.

Graham and his men were not a patient lot, saying "Two nights and two days a waitin' on them baars was enough." Graham gave his own ultimatum and when that went unanswered, he gave the order to fire a four pound cannon ball at the mansion. That single cannon ball, dear reader, that made a rather clean arc through the air, hitting and crashing through the Mansion's tile roof, marked the beginning and the end of the "Siege of Monterey". Nicholas Guiterrez had seen enough battle and surrendered after the one shot.

There were a few additional but minor altercations with the southern Californios that disagreed with the resolutions passed by Alvarado, Graham's presence brought them back in line without any bloodshed. Alvarado's cousin and friend Jose Castro was sent to Mexico's mainland capital to announce the takeover of Alta California from the Mexican government. President Bustamante had a depleted army from the battles over Texas and was ill prepared to regain control of the large territory. When Jose Castro arrived he came to the President with different news. Jose informed him that his partner Alvarado was giving the territory back to Mexico under the condition that Alvarado be seated as the new Governor of Alta California. President Bustamante agreed.

After everything was said and done, Alvarado's new leadership really didn't make any real reform for either the Californios or the Yankees. This didn't sit well with either group; both felt duped by what Alvarado had done and were especially upset with Graham and his men for not doing more. Alvarado used this unrest to his advantage to deflect the issues at hand entirely on Graham and his fellow Rifleros.

The Graham Affair

What happened next led to an international crisis between the United States, England and Mexico called the Graham Affair. The following is a tale of horrific torture, suffering and in the end, vindication of sorts. The Graham Affair also cast a light on the vulnerability of Mexico to maintain order in Alta California, giving the United States an indication that the territory could be easily secured into the Union with the proper strategy.

The so-called Graham Affair began on the moonless night of April 6, 1840. Alvarado felt that Graham was planning a revolt under the guise of a horse race Isaac was planning with fellow horse owners in Los Angeles and San Diego. That was enough for him to gather forces to arrest Graham and many of the other Yankees in the area.

While the men were actually arrested in the end, from Graham's own telling, his intended fate was far worse:

"We slept quietly, until about three o'clock in the morning, when I was awakened by the discharge of a pistol near my head, the ball of which passed through the handkerchief about my neck. I sprang to my feet, and jumped in the direction of the villains, when they discharged six other pistols, so near me that my shirt took fire...but the trepidation of the cowards prevented their taking good aim; for only one of their shots took effect, and that in my left arm.

"After firing they fell back a few paces and commenced reloading their pieces. I perceived by the light of their pistols that they were too numerous for a single man to contend with, and determined to escape. But I had scarcely got six paces from the door when I was overtaken and assailed with heavy blows from their swords. These I succeeded in parrying off to such an extent that I was not much injured by them. Being incensed at last by my successful resistance, they grappled with me, and threw me down, when an ensign by the name of Joaquin Terres drew his dirk, and saying with an oath that he would let out my life, made a thrust at my heart. God saved me again. The weapon passing between my body and left arm, sunk deep in the ground; and before he had an opportunity of repeating his blow they dragged me up the hill in the rear of my house, where Jose Castro was standing. They called to him. 'Here he is! here he is!' whereupon Castro rode up and struck me with the back of his sword over the head so severely as to bring me to the ground; and then ordered four balls to be put through me. But this was prevented by a faithful Indian in my service, who threw himself on me, declaring that he would receive the balls in his own heart!

"Unwilling to be thwarted, however, in their design to destroy me, they next fastened a rope to one of my arms, and passed it to a man on horseback, who wound it firmly around the horn of his saddle. Then the rest of them, taking hold of the other arm, endeavored to haul my shoulders out of joint; But the rope broke. Thinking the scoundrels bent on killing me in some way, I begged for liberty to commend my soul to god. To this they replied. 'You shall never pray till you kneel over your grave.' They then conducted me to my house and permitted me to put on my pantaloons. While there, they asked where Mr. Morris was. I told them I did not know. They then put their lances to my breast and told me to call him or die. I answered that he had made his escape. While I was saying this, Mr. Neal came to the house, pale from loss of blood and vomiting terribly. He had had a lance thrust through his thigh, and a deep wound in his leg, which nearly separated the cord of the heel.

"They next put Mr. Neal and myself in double irons, carried us half a mile into the plain, left us under guard, and returned to plunder the house. After having been absent a short time, they came and conducted us back to our rifled home. As soon as we arrived there, a man by the name of Manuel Larias approached me with a drawn sword, and commanded me to inform him where my money was buried. I told him I had none. He cursed me and turned

away. I had some deposited in the ground, but I determined they should never enjoy it. After having robbed me of my books and papers, which were all the evidence I had that these scoundrels and others were largely indebted to me, and having taken whatever was valuable on my premises, and distributed it among themselves, they proceeded to take an inventory of what was left, as it were the whole of my property; and then put me on horseback and sent to this prison. You know the rest. I am chained like a dog, and suffer like one."

Graham and 46 other men were taken to a small adobe jail cell in Monterey. The cell itself was so crowded that the men were forced to take turns to lie down to sleep while the rest of the men had to stand and wait for a turn. During this time and in fact for the duration, the captives were treated horribly. There were cases of compassion to at least treat the captives humanly, but these small acts came only after much pleading by fellow Yankees.

On April 23, 1840, the prisoners were marched to Alvarado's home where one by one, each was asked to stand trial. Alvarado asked each to produce their passport and since most were apprehended from their beds or had their passports confiscated were declared to being in the country illegally.

The prisoners, 23 Englishman, 23 Yankees and Graham were sentenced with conspiracy and were transported to the lower deck of a ship that ultimately took them to a prison in Tepic, Mexico. During this time, the guards gave the men only enough food to keep the captives alive. To keep their spirits up, the men sang the Star Spangled Banner and Rule Britannia until Jose Castro, who was sent along to escort the men issued an order that the next man who sang would be stabbed to death.

The ship landed in San Blas and the prisoners were placed in a jail for three days where again they were given no food or water. Then barefoot and shackled limb to limb in chains, they were forced to march 60 miles to the inland town of Tepic.

Things changed due in part to one man, a lawyer who had arrived in Monterey just the day before the first arrests by the name of Thomas Jefferson Farnham. Thomas defended the prisoners, even as far as to meet them in Mexico to lobby for improved treatment. The United States sent a ship to Monterey to investigate the matter and the Mexican government launched a formal investigation of their own on the incident. They even went as far as to arrest Jose Castro and he was tried for Court Marshall by the Mexican Government on the basis of cruelty. Jose Castro was found not guilty.

In the end, while some men were released sooner, Isaac Graham and nineteen other men did not return to Monterey, California until July 20, 1841, over a year since their initial arrest. They were all found to be innocent of all charges, given full passports and a fair amount of money as retribution for the cruelties and hardships that had endured.

Around this same period Isaac Graham's friend Joseph Majors was granted Rancho Zayante by none other than Governor Juan Alvarado. Majors then turned around and sold the Rancho to Graham, though under the law of the Mexican government, the land was still owned by Majors. Graham later petitioned that the land be put officially under his name in 1843, however, since he was not a Mexican citizen, the request was denied.

California's First Power Sawmill and Final Years

Issac Graham formed a partnership with Naile, the other man captured the first night of the Graham Affair, along with William Ware, Frederick Hoegel and Peter Lassen. They built what became the first water powered sawmill in California, located where the Roaring Camp Railroad stands today. He built a road from the sawmill to Branciforte, which today is referred to as Graham Hill Road. Graham continued with his practice of making whiskey which only added to the rowdy atmosphere and the operation's reputation as a "wild and roaring camp".

At 45 Isaac courted and married Tallatha Catherine Bennett who at 21, lived with her mom Mary Bennett on a ranch near Love Creek. Ms. Bennett went by her middle name Catherine. They married on Graham's ranch informally and without a proper minster to make the marriage truly official. One year into marriage the two had a daughter who they named Matilda Jane.

Despite these wondrous events the remainder of Graham's life was a mixture of happiness and devastation. In the same year as his daughter's birth, one of his best friends, business partner and fellow patriot Henry Naile was shot in cold blood and killed over a land dispute. The killer was found not guilty due to self-defense and in fact, Isaac was himself put to blame for his friend's death due to his own reckless nature. A total of 21 citizens wrote a petition condemning Graham, including Joseph Majors, the man who sold Graham the Rancho Zayante and originally travelled from the east with Isaac. The petition stated that Graham:

"...is perpetually corrupting the peace of our vicinity and for the last six years has not ceased to invite or attempt revolutions, challenges for duels, assassinations, and disobedience of the laws even to the extent of arming himself when summoned....We are unanimously of the opinion that said Graham has been the sole cause of the death of his companion Henry Naile through the many compromises into which he had been led by this dissolute man Graham."

His rebellious ways were catching up to him; however Graham did try to settle down somewhat and even tried an unsuccessful attempt at politics. In 1849 his estranged son Jesse Jones Graham reunited himself with his dad much to Graham's delight, some twenty years after Graham's first wife took Jesse Jones away from him. That same year, Graham had a second daughter named Amanda Anne.

Then in 1850 his wife gave birth to a third child who was stillborn. A single day after the tragedy, Isaac and his new found son went to San Jose on extended business. When he came back, he found Catherine, his daughters and his cache of gold gone.

Catherine was rightfully upset that Graham would leave so soon after their child's death. Graham chased her down and eventually found her in Oregon and took the children back. They both sued each other multiple times, the unofficial marriage was dragged into the matter and Catherine's name was tarnished as an adulteress while Graham was painted as a murderer. In the end, Graham's marriage was deemed legitimate by no less that the State Supreme Court and the children would remain in Isaac's custody. Perhaps the worst of this period is with Graham's son Jesse, who got in an argument with Catherine's family and then killed her brother Daniel and wounded her mother. Jesse was forced to become a fugitive and was not caught for another thirty eight years.

At 64, Isaac Graham passed away while on a trip to San Francisco. His body was brought back to Santa Cruz where he was laid to rest next to his second daughter Amanda Anne who had passed away earlier that year at the age of 14. They are buried to this day side by side at the Evergreen Cemetery in Santa Cruz. Catherine Bennett went on to remarry and have six children. Isaac's fugitive son Jesse was caught, tried and found not guilty and lived a long life. As for Isaac Graham, his role in California history would fade to the legacy of a two lane road that bears his name, nothing more than the eastern border of Henry Cowell Redwoods State Park.

Henry Cowell

The Brother's Cowell Head West

Henry Cowell was born in the town of Wrentham, Massachusetts on June 30, 1819. Wrentham was and still is a small town full of New England charm and itself was established back in 1673.

Cowell came out west during the gold rush and while it is not clear the exact year he made the trip from Wrentham, it is known that Cowell brought along his brother John and that the two were in their 30's at the time. Henry left a farmer's life and a farm that had been in the family for over 100 years. While he would leave the farm, the heritage of farming would not leave him. On local Santa Cruz census reports he listed "farmer" as his occupation well after his success as a lime entrepreneur.

John and Henry likely tried their luck trying to find riches in the gold fields of the Sierras. Like many who stayed and thrived, they found success offering a service or product that aided in the mining of gold rather than finding gold itself. John and Henry found ample success in the rather straight forward business of drayage and storage in San Francisco. They stored and transfered cargo from incoming ships to their destinations and built the business to include its own wharf and warehouse.

The Cowell's brother's luck was about to change, at first for the worse, but in the long run to their advantage. The city of San Francisco at this time was built rapidly to support the gold miners. As lumber was in plentiful supply, most buildings at this time were made of wood. The tremendous rate of growth gave room for error and four fires had already swept through the city. On May 4, 1851, exactly one year from the fourth devastating San Francisco fire, a fifth broke out.

The fire started at 11pm the night before and quickly consumed the Business District. Reports tell that the fire was so hot that water evaporated as steam. The fire traveled under the hallowed spaces underneath the plank sidewalks travelling quickly from one block to the next. In the end, three fourths of the city of San Francisco was lost. Equally as amazing, the residents of San Francisco rebuilt one fifth of it back in just ten days.

Lime Workers

While this did set the two brothers back in their drayage business, they would recover. The fires also created an atmosphere of change in building material. Instead of wood, folks decided to use brick. Brick homes needed mortar and mortar at the time contained one essential ingredient, lime. Lime was an expensive material however, as it was imported, coming all the way around Cape Horn to its destination in San Francisco. A cheaper source of the material was needed.

Henry headed back briefly to Massachusetts in 1854 to marry Harriet Carpenter. They returned to San Francisco and ultimately raised a family of six children. The first, Roland died shortly after birth; however their other five, Ernest Victor, Isabella Marion, Samuel Henry, Sarah Elizabeth and Helen Edith survived to adulthood.

Lime Builds a Strong Business Empire

It's here that we should introduce two other gold rush adventurers who like the brothers Cowell, found no luck finding gold, but did find luck with California's other riches. The men were Albion P. Jordan and Isaac E. Davis. The two arrived in California in 1850 and found themselves working on a steamboat that paddled up the delta between San Francisco and Sacramento. By accident, the two men found some limestone near Mt. Diablo. They burned the rock in the steamboat's furnace and found it to produce a high quality grade of lime. The two men up and quit their steamboat positions and established what would become the largest lime manufacturing operation in California. That business was called Jordan and Davis, located in the Santa Cruz Mountains. Since this is a story about Henry Cowell and his lime company, the reader may see why there was an introduction of Jordan and Davis. Before going further though, what the heck is lime?

While the process for making lime and its use is amongst the oldest in the chronicles of human civilization, dating back some seven thousand years, most of us modern wanderers have no idea how to make it or why you would want to. Lime is made by heating limestone, marble or any raw material containing calcium carbonate to 1640° F. Doing so drives out the carbon dioxide; leaving lime, (calcium hydroxide) a white, caustic material that acts violently with water. Lime as a word was originally a term for "stickiness", which is appropriate since if you add lime with sand and then add water, you get mortar. Prior to the invention of Portland cement beginning in 1824, lime based mortar was the standard stuff put between bricks for buildings in San Francisco and elsewhere. As well, a thinner mixture was used as plaster.

The lime industry of Santa Cruz was eventually shut down due to the scarcity of cheap local firewood. It took a lot of redwood to bake each batch of lime. It simply became harder to come by that much wood cheaply as the forests were consumed. The British invention of Portland cement had an impact too, which remains the standard for making concrete even today. However, though it was invented early in the 1800's it took over 90 years for Portland cement to completely take hold of the mortar industry. Lime production in

Cowell Limes Works ca. 1889

Santa Cruz was widespread until the early 1900's. Most of it was shipped to San Francisco by schooners where it was then transported by land to help stand up the many gold mining towns in California.

The process for making lime was fairly simple. A "Blaster" blew up the rock from the limestone quarry. Then several men took sledgehammers to the rock, creating manageable pieces the size of a melon. The stone was carried by wagons on a makeshift rail system to the kilns. Once loaded, the kiln was heated for four days and required between 70-140 cords of wood. It was then allowed to cool for two days and the newly produced lime was loaded into barrels and transported down to waiting schooners.

Loading the Lime Barrels

Going back to the story of Henry and John Cowell, their drayage business was a financial success. For Henry though, it was not enough. His brother John headed back east due to poor health. Henry decided to get into the lime business himself and purchased Jordan's share of the Jordan and Davis lime business in 1865 for $100,000 when Jordan became too ill to continue the partnership. Henry moved his family down to Santa Cruz and the lime company was renamed Davis and Cowell. He continued to be well tied into the relationships he had built in San Francisco and eventually moved back to the city later in life. For the next 32 years however, Santa Cruz became the town Cowell would call home.

In 1888 Isaac Davis died and Henry purchased the other half of the business for $400,000. By the early 1900's Henry purchased and operated four lime kiln operations within Santa Cruz County, including the Adams Lime Kiln within what is now Wilder Ranch State Park. Cowell's operation was end to end, from providing fuel for the lime kilns, a barrel cooperage to transport the lime and even ships to transport it to San Francisco for distribution. Henry Cowell employed 175 men in total as of 1897. He paid them but once a year, making a trip to San Francisco for the $100,000 payroll amount, working through the night with his paymaster and paying the men the following day.

Henry reinvested his fortunes into real estate and had an equal business instinct for good land. He purchased holdings along the coast near San Luis Obispo to the south and as far north as Canada. His holdings were spread over an impressive 14 counties as well as prime lots along Market Street and the present day Embarcadero in San Francisco.

Henry Cowell

Henry Cowell – The Person

Henry Cowell was a shrewd businessman which served him well financially but would put him at odds when it came to relationships. One example of this was with the Adams Lime Kilns owned by Samuel Adams. Adams was forced to take a longer route and create his own port near Old Man's Bluff within Wilder Ranch State Park. His operation was very close to a shorter route to the main Santa Cruz port but it required access through Cowell's land. Cowell denied him the access and ultimately purchased the Adam's Kiln operation.

Henry Cowell was also a shy and protective man. He went out of his way to avoid the media and most of what is known of him is through public business records and witness accounts than through his own writings. It is safe to say he hated publicity going to great lengths to avoid being in the spotlight.

He raised smart athletic children, the boys excelled in sports and the girls were noted in the top of their classes. This focus however did not expand to relationships as Cowell was concerned that outsiders were only interested in getting their hands on the family money.

This protectiveness was shown early on as it became well known that the girls were off limits at school for courting. The rigidity went into adulthood and even marriage became an issue. Only one Cowell child married. Ernest Cowell married a young girl from Boston named Alice Maud Bovyer. Henry Cowell became outraged at this marriage and went as far as to temporarily disown his own son. Ernest eventually left his wife and returned to Santa Cruz to run the family business until his death. None of the other four children would marry, which in a way became a major catalyst for the creation of this State Park, given there were no heirs created from any of Henry's children.

The Fateful Year of 1903

The Two Sisters

In 1903 Henry Cowell at age 84 was the richest man in Santa Cruz. His children were fully grown, Sarah being 40 years of age. The year would become a major milestone of tragedy for the Cowell's. Henry was shot in the shoulder over a long standing boundary dispute with D. Leigh Ingalsbe. Not much is known about this incident but does cause one to wonder what provoked the shooting of an 84 year old.

Henry was shot in March 1903 and was looking as if he would make a full recovery. In May of the same year, his daughter Sarah was thrown from a horse drawn buggy and died within an hour of the accident. Apparently the horse bolted. Her hat was found a half mile from where she was thrown. The accident occurred on the Cowell Ranch, now the campus of the University of California, Santa Cruz. Since her death, there have been multiple sightings of Sarah's ghost in an area known as Haunted Meadow.

The death of Sarah was a blow to the family. Henry Cowell passed in August of 1903. The remaining daughters Isabella and Helen refused to set foot on the ranch from the day of her death onwards. The two became a pair of recluses, living in a family owned mansion in Atherton. Helen died first in 1932 at the age of 66. Upon her death Isabella ordered the supports that held up the Atherton house pulled out and a wire fence put around the property. The house toppled over and sat in a demolished state for many years behind a locked gate, though the gardeners were retained to keep the grounds around the ruin as lovely as they had been kept prior.

Henry Cowell's will was another enigma. It listed the executor of the will as his daughter Helen and the beneficiary as the Henry Cowell Lime and Cement Company. However the first two sheets where the bequests should be listed were left blank. Since the children had joint ownership in the company, the assets were left to them.

Son Ernest Takes Over the Business

Ernest took over the day to day management of the business. As much as one catastrophe catalyzed the growth of the lime operations, another was one of the causes for its decline. The San Francisco earthquake of 1906 caused the company to lose most of its holdings within the city itself, with the Cowell Company's building, another ten story building and a lime warehouse destroyed in the quake and subsequent fire.

While this created a short term growth spurt for the company, it signaled a longer term change in building design. Brick buildings were not the best choice in earthquake country and architects returned to other choices, including using wood framed homes. Another longer term decline trend was in mortar itself. It was being replaced by a stronger invention, Portland Cement. Portland Cement would become a standard in material construction that not only would replace mortar but would remain in use to present day.

There was one more factor in the decline of lime production in Santa Cruz, lack of cheap fuel. The forests had been cut down and while the operations retrofitted to use oil to fuel the kilns, the extra cost ate into the profits.

Ernest died at the age of 53 in 1911, just five years after the San Francisco earthquake. His will had three noteworthy components, all regarding his generosity. It carried a bequest to each employee of the Henry Cowell Lime and Cement Company of $500-$1000 depending on tenure. He also set up a $10,000 trust for scholarships within the University of California system. In addition he gave the bulk of his estate for the funding of a major campus building at the University of California Berkeley which ultimately led to the creation of the Ernest V. Cowell Student Health Center as well as major funding for the men's gymnasium.

Final Years under Samuel Harry Cowell

Samuel (aka Harry) was next to stand up to take over the family business. He continued to run the lime operations but shifted additional focus to horse breeding. Harry was a big fan of all animals and it was witnessed that the Cowell Ranch was amok with cats, dogs, peacocks, turkeys, horses, lambs, chickens and even tame quail. Each animal was well-cared for and each had a name. He bred some of the finest race horses in California at the time.

His love of animals extended to an equal love for the land. He took a personal interest in inspecting the Cowell Ranch on his visits. He had the annual burn of the brush within the ranch discontinued and allowed it to return to its native state. The wharf and its corresponding warehouse were no longer needed as the railroad replaced ocean transport. He deeded the old wharf and the land owned to the City of Santa Cruz, who named it Cowell Beach.

Samuel Harry Cowell

Harry ran the final years of the company at a loss, but did so to keep the employees on payroll. He awoke at 6am each morning to have breakfast in the cookhouse with the men. It was said he never let a man go and was well praised by his employees.

Isabella died at age 92 in 1950. She left a million dollars to the Helen Cowell Children's Hospital in Sacramento. The M. H. de Young Museum received both her jade and art collection. Again she wanted her home demolished and stipulated that her $5.5 million estate on Jackson Street in San Francisco be torn down. Harry lived in the same mansion at the time and really enjoyed the place. He kept the mansion and donated the value of the estate to the Old People's Home which then stood on the corner of Pine and Pierce Streets.

Harry remained the sole heir of the Cowell fortune for the next four years, passing on at the age of 93 in 1955. Just two years prior to his death he performed his legacy moment, creating the Henry Cowell Redwoods State Park. The act was not just a simple transfer; it required a series of events that had to work themselves out properly, the largest of which being that the adjoining Welch's Big Tree Grove be included into the State Park. This was no easy task since the Cowell family did not own this portion of the park. It took a series of events, the right timing, coupled with the generosity of Samuel Harry Cowell to bring the State Park together. The park is now enjoyed by some 750,000 visitors each year and the Big Grove aside, many parts of the park are still healing from a time of industrial might over preservation. With a few more generations of stewardship, this gift of Harry Cowell and the State will allow the area to return to something closer to what the Ohlone might have seen before the Spaniard, Californio and Yankee came to this land.

At his death, the remainder of the Cowell heir went to various sizeable bequests. The Cowell Ranch became the land for U. C. Santa Cruz. The S.H. Cowell Foundation, a nonprofit funding a number of philanthropic activities, was established to continue his generosity. At the time, the amount used to establish the foundation was estimated at $14 million. He also made many other bequests, recipients including Stanford University, Mills College and the San Francisco Academy of Sciences.

Cowell lime Works ca 1962. Ansel Adams

Welch's Big Tree Grove

Catalyst of the First State Park

Probably the most interesting thing about Welch's Big Tree Grove is that in a way it was the initial catalyst for the creation of all California State Parks. This is not to say that another series of events wouldn't have led to the preservation of some of California's greatest lands for generations to enjoy, but the roots of the State Park system do trace back to Welch's Big Tree Grove.

Joseph Welch came to Santa Cruz to mine the "red gold" of the redwood forest not as fuel for lime kilns or lumber for homes but as an attraction unto themselves. He purchased a small but uncut portion of the Rancho Zayante in 1867 from Edward Stanly. Within the 40 acre parcel of old growth coastal redwoods he built a simple train station that would carry passengers from San Francisco 74 miles north. Next to the train station, which was established in 1879, he built a high end hotel, dining hall, single cabin "suites", a dance pavilion and a clubhouse. The traveler stepped off the train to within walking distance of every amenity a tourist would want for a pleasant and relaxing stay. There was superb fishing, fresh air, even a honeymoon suite in the hollow of a tree, all nestled amongst what became known as simply the Big Trees.

By the late 1890's the Welch's Big Tree Grove became an internationally famous tourist destination. Nearly every visitor that came to San Francisco looked at how they could fit in the train ride down to experience the Big Trees. The resort complex was a go to destination for many and even hosted the visits of two presidents, a handful of governors and other celebrities.

The British published Wide World Magazine wanted to do a piece on the Big Trees and commissioned local photographer and painter Andrew Putnam Hill to take the photos for their article. Little did Andrew know this visit to the Welch's Big Tree Grove became the beginning of the preservationist movement and ultimately, his legacy.

Andrew Putnam Hill

Andrew came to California with his uncle at the age of fourteen and took up studies at the Catholic Santa Clara College (now known as Santa Clara University). He opened a portrait painting studio in 1876 along with another painter Louis Lussier. As a descendent of early American settlers, his paintings played with both pioneer and natural landscape themes. He became one of California's foremost painters, with pieces exhibited in the state capital and as part of other permanent exhibits.

Andrew Putnam Hill

While amassing a fine reputation as a painter, Andrew was developing an equal reputation for his photography. With photos and illustrations carried in magazines worldwide, it was easy to see why in 1899, he was asked to photograph Welch's redwoods for a British magazine. He loaded up his gear and took the train to the Big Trees, but left without a single photograph. As he was setting up his camera, the Big Trees owner Joseph Welch himself refused to let him photograph "Welch's Trees" for commercial use without receiving payment. Said Hill of the event:

"I was a little angry, and somewhat disgusted, with my reception at the Santa Cruz Big Trees. It made me think. There were still fifteen minutes until the train time. Just as the gate closed, the thought flashed through my mind that these trees, because of their size and antiquity, were among the natural wonders of the world, and should be saved for posterity. I said to myself, "I will start a campaign immediately to make a public park of the place." I argued that as I had been furnishing illustrations for a number of writers, whom I knew quite well, that there was a latent force, which, when awakened to a noble cause, would immediately respond, and perhaps arouse the press of the whole country. Thus was born my idea of saving the redwoods."

The Original Sempervirens Club, 1900

This visit sparked the foundation of the Sempervirens Club, California's oldest land conservation organization. The club took on the role of preserving the majestic coastal redwood (*Sequoia sempervirens*) and their strategy was to rally up funds to purchase land and then transfer it to the state or local agency to create parks for public use. While their intentions began with Welch's Big Tree Grove they quickly focused on the larger grove of redwoods in Big Basin. Within two years of creating the Club, Big Basin Redwoods State Park became the state of California's first example of what is today a system of 280 state parks set aside for all to enjoy.

Within the focus of the mighty coastal redwood itself, Andrew P. Hill began an effort of conservation at a time when only 25% of the old growth redwoods remained. He died a poor man, leaving little financially to his heirs. However, his initial acts of conservation have created state parks that together preserve much of the last 3-5% of these old growth "natural wonders". His legacy and his efforts will forever be associated with the preservation of the tallest trees in the world for future generations.

The End Story of Welch's Big Tree Grove

Joseph Welch should get some credit, he did purchase a large grove of coastal redwoods for ecotourism rather than outright logging and it was certainly in his right to not want his "assets" to be taken advantage of monetarily. He too did bring focus to the giant redwood by creating an environment suitable for presidential visits as well as worldwide attention to the trees. However, his quest to blend business with preservation would ultimately not serve him well.

In May 1903 President Theodore Roosevelt visited the Big Trees Grove. He saw dozens of business and personal cards pinned as a form of graffiti on one old growth redwood. The President strongly disapproved of this practice and even gave a lecture on the "evils of vandalism". While the cards were promptly removed, with Big Basin State Park becoming the new big tree attraction, the heyday of Welch's Big Trees Grove was coming to an end.

The Welch's looked for a buyer of the grove and found one in 1930 when it was purchased by the County of Santa Cruz, paying $75,000 for the 120 acres including the 40 acres of Big Trees. In 1952 Samuel Harry Cowell started a campaign to convince the County to deed the grove and adjoining land to the State. In return, he would add his larger surrounding acres to create Henry Cowell Redwoods State Park. With much negotiation, he was able to achieve his goal and the park bearing his father's name opened on August 18, 1954.

John Frémont

While Frémont's part in the historical saga of Henry Cowell Redwoods State Park is brief, this guide wouldn't be complete without a short description of the man. For his part in the park itself, legend has it he slept in the hollow of one of the large old growth redwood trees in late 1846. The "Fremont Tree" still stands today and can be found along the Redwood Grove Loop. Disputed legends aside, John Frémont did visit the Big Trees in 1888 with his wife.

Historically Frémont's career as a military and political figure was mixed. He was born into social prominence, related distantly to George Washington as well as Col. Thomas Whiting.

He was born on January 21, 1813 out of wedlock, the product of his mother and her French tutor turned lover and a husband who refused to give his wife a divorce.

As a young man, John Fremon changed his last name to Frémont, married the daughter of Thomas Hart Benton, who was the leader of an expansionist movement called Manifest Destiny. With Kit Carson, Frémont helped his father-in-law's movement by leading survey expeditions in the West. John Frémont became the first U.S. citizen to see Lake Tahoe and mapped many of the major geographic features of the West, including Mount St. Helens and the Great Basin.

His findings were summarized in a Congressional report titled "Report and Map". It would become the map for pioneers to Oregon and California during the mid-1840's through the Gold Rush period. Whether used outright or the report's findings rewritten into other publications, this traveler's guide had also accomplished its goal as a government publication to expand the US territories farther west.

Frémont in front of The Fremont Tree

It was early in 1846 that John Frémont made his way to Jose Castro in Monterey to provoke a conflict, camping at the summit of current Fremont Peak. The conflict with Castro never materialized. Realizing he was outnumbered he backed off and his small expedition of 55 men moved north to the friendly Oregonian Territory of Klamath Lake. In May 1846 he saved Kit Carson from an Indian attack along the lake. This is timeframe it is thought that Frémont slept in the Fremont tree.

In June 1846 Frémont returned to the Mexican owned California and camp at the San Rafael Mission. He sent three of his men, one of which was Kit Carson, to confront three Californios that were disembarking from a boat at Point San Pedro. He ordered three shots and killed them, stating, "I have got no room for prisoners". The three were well respected Dons and were either Alcalde's (Governors) themselves or were directly connected to an Alcalde. This shooting was later used against John Frémont in 1856 when he ran for president against John Buchanan.

Frémont played an important role during the Mexican-American War, helping capture Santa Barbara with a troop of 300 men. He led his men south to capture Los Angeles and obtain the surrender of the Mexican Governor Andrés Pico who ended the war with the signing of the Treaty of Cahuenga. While the war lasted only a year and a half, the heavy number of casualties, high cost and most importantly, Frémont's stance against slavery created a tremendous political aftermath. Frémont was charged with mutiny and assumption of powers. His trial ended in a court martial (and then an immediate presidential pardon for services rendered).

Frémont returned to California, which was now a state and successfully became one of the State's first two senators. During the Civil War he again led controversially as the commander of the Army's Department of the West. Here he assumed powers that he did not have and President Lincoln himself relieved General Frémont of his command in 1861. Interestingly, he later ran against Lincoln during Lincoln's second run for office. The Republican Party itself split into two factions, the split party calling themselves the Radical Republicans who stood up Frémont as their man. The movement was short-lived and Lincoln got his second term as president.

From here, Frémont's role in history dissolved for the most part into one of a private citizen with the occasional public appearance. He passed on at the age of 77 in New York City on July 13, 1890, two years after visiting the now famous Frémont Tree. Frémont is a bit of a case study amongst historians, here was a man of presidential caliber but ultimately became his own worst enemy. Theories abound both as to why he was so self-destructive as well as what would have become of the Civil War and US history in general if he had of succeeded in his run at presidency.

Geology

Santa Cruz Sandhills on Ridge Fire Road

Geological theories abound on how all the mountains within the western edge of North American were created, with two being the most prevalent. One suggests a process similar to a conveyer belt of earth being pushed eastward across the Pacific and finally landing at the continent of North America. Like boxes that pile up at the end of an unmanned conveyer belt, so too the Farallon Plate would bunch up the land, creating the Rockies, Sierras and the myriad of smaller mountain ranges such as California's Coastal Range.

The thing is, the land mass that makes up essentially the western quarter of North America is made up of dozens of different types of crust and trying to piece the real story is far more complicated. The latest theories expand on the "conveyer belt" theory, stating essentially that there were multiple conveyer belts at play, that some came before the Farallon Plate and even moved land westward rather than eastward. The result is the western North American continent is a mash-up of multiple forces and the not the singular continuous action of one lone plate.

Whatever the reality is may never truly be known, the geology is that complicated. What is known is that for Henry Cowell, it is part of the Coastal Range of California and its principle body of water, the San Lorenzo River is following an ancient earthquake fault known as the Ben Lomond Fault. When it was active, something it hasn't been in over 80,000 years, the Ben Lomond Fault was at one point under the waters of the Pacific which were farther inland than they are today. This marine intrusion deposited a shallow layer of marine sands which are collectively known as the Santa Cruz Sandhills.

As the ocean's waters receded, plants that could thrive in the low nutrient sands and established themselves on the dunes. The sand slowly became soil different from the surrounding areas, creating what are called "biological islands", an ecosystem that is unique and unto itself. These are not islands separated by water, but by a different ecological environment. This area contains the so called Zayante Soils, derived first from sediments deposited over 15 million years ago and built into soil by the continued detritus of plants that lived and died to help build this soil.

The Zayante soils don't hold water well and are low in nutrients. They do however support life that can survive and sometimes even thrive in this type of environment. The moisture loving coastal redwood is not found here. What is found are four different plant species and three animal species found nowhere else in the world along with a large variety of plants and animals at home in the similarly challenged chaparral ecosystem.

One aspect noted in several portions of the park is the steep terrain. There are two major forces shaping the land in the Santa Cruz Mountains, erosion and earthquakes. The earth is uplifted by the quakes and then shaped by the erosion of water and wind over vast amounts of time. On a geologic timescale, the uplift of the earth is occurring faster than the wind and water can smooth out the terrain. While water and wind have done a fair job at rounding the edges at it were, the many earthquakes and resultant sharp uplifting of the earth appears to be winning for now.

The other reason for the steepness is the soil and rock itself. Built from marine deposits for the most part and not given the pressure or heat to become the harder more brittle stone found further inland, the sandstones of Cowell tend to cleave sharply as landslides rather than break off in brittle pieces a bit at a time. If you have ever built a sand castle and watched a portion of the tower cleave off at a sharp angle, the process is similar, only on a grander scale. This is magnified by the earthquakes which of course give the hills a good shaking and help the ground to cleave.

Trails in the Main Unit

Henry Cowell Redwoods State Park has two full sections that can be explored. To make life easier for the reader, the trails are divided amongst these two sections, namely the Main Unit (or what everyone thinks of when they hear of Henry Cowell Redwoods State Park) and the Fall Creek Unit. Both sections have much to offer and are different in their own ways.

For purposes of describing the Main Unit of the park, the trails are divided into three sections:

- Trails near the main parking area
- Trails near the San Lorenzo River
- Trails near the Henry Cowell Campground.

As in any attempt to organize a bunch of trails, one odd ball trail doesn't fit well in the schema devised. For Henry Cowell Redwoods State Park, this would be the Pipeline Road which traverses all three sections. The Pipeline Road description can be found in the section of trails near the main parking area.

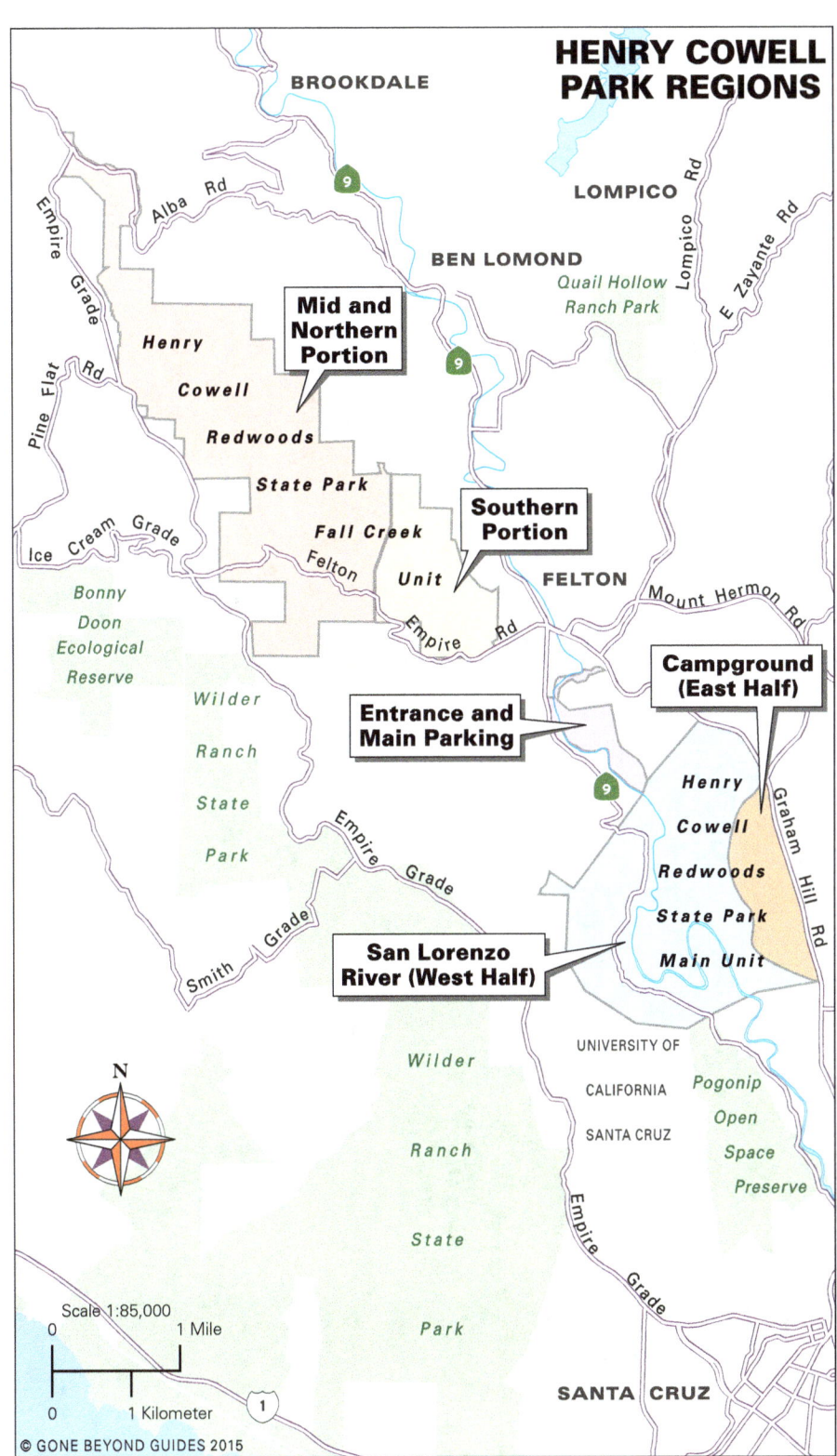

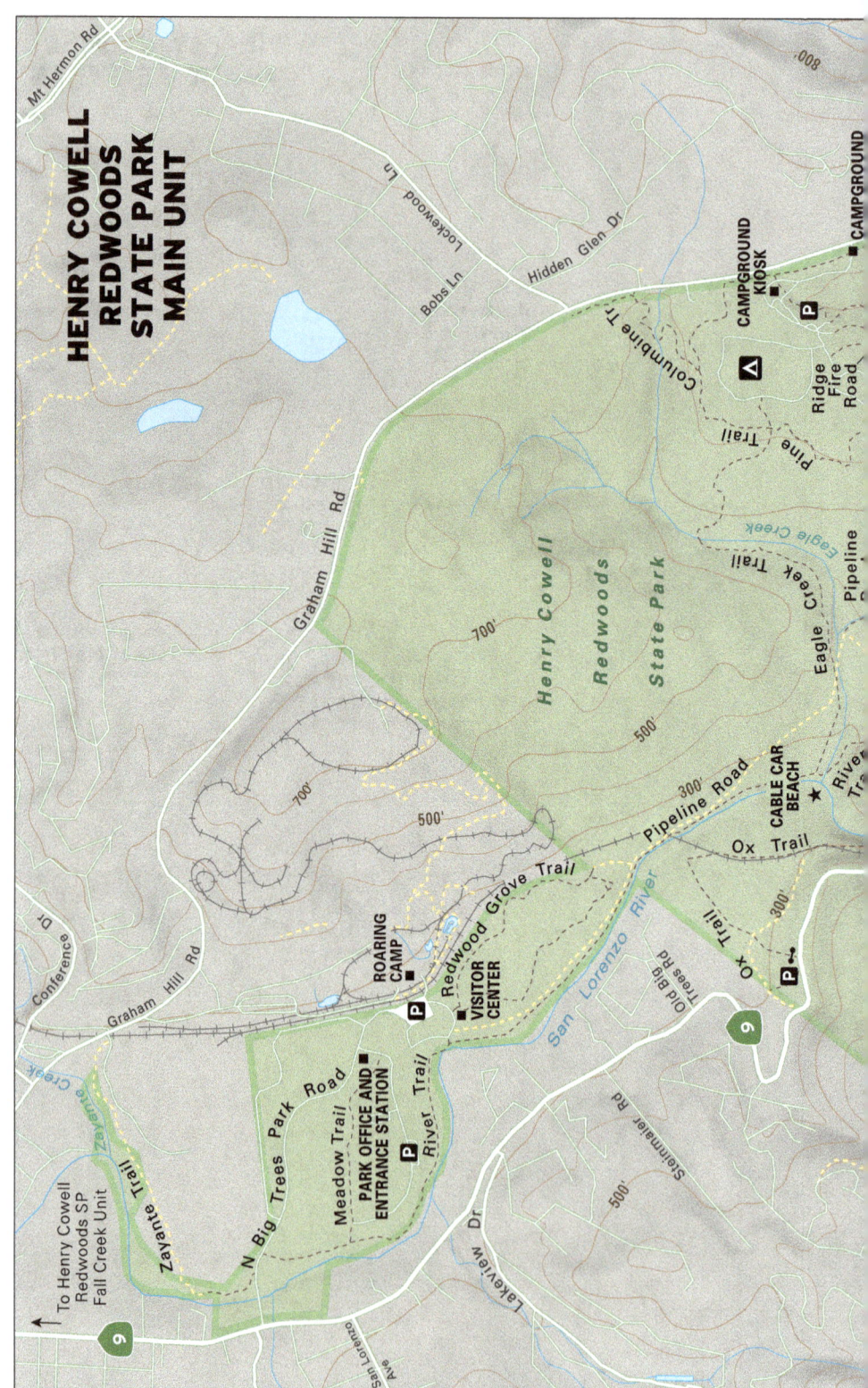

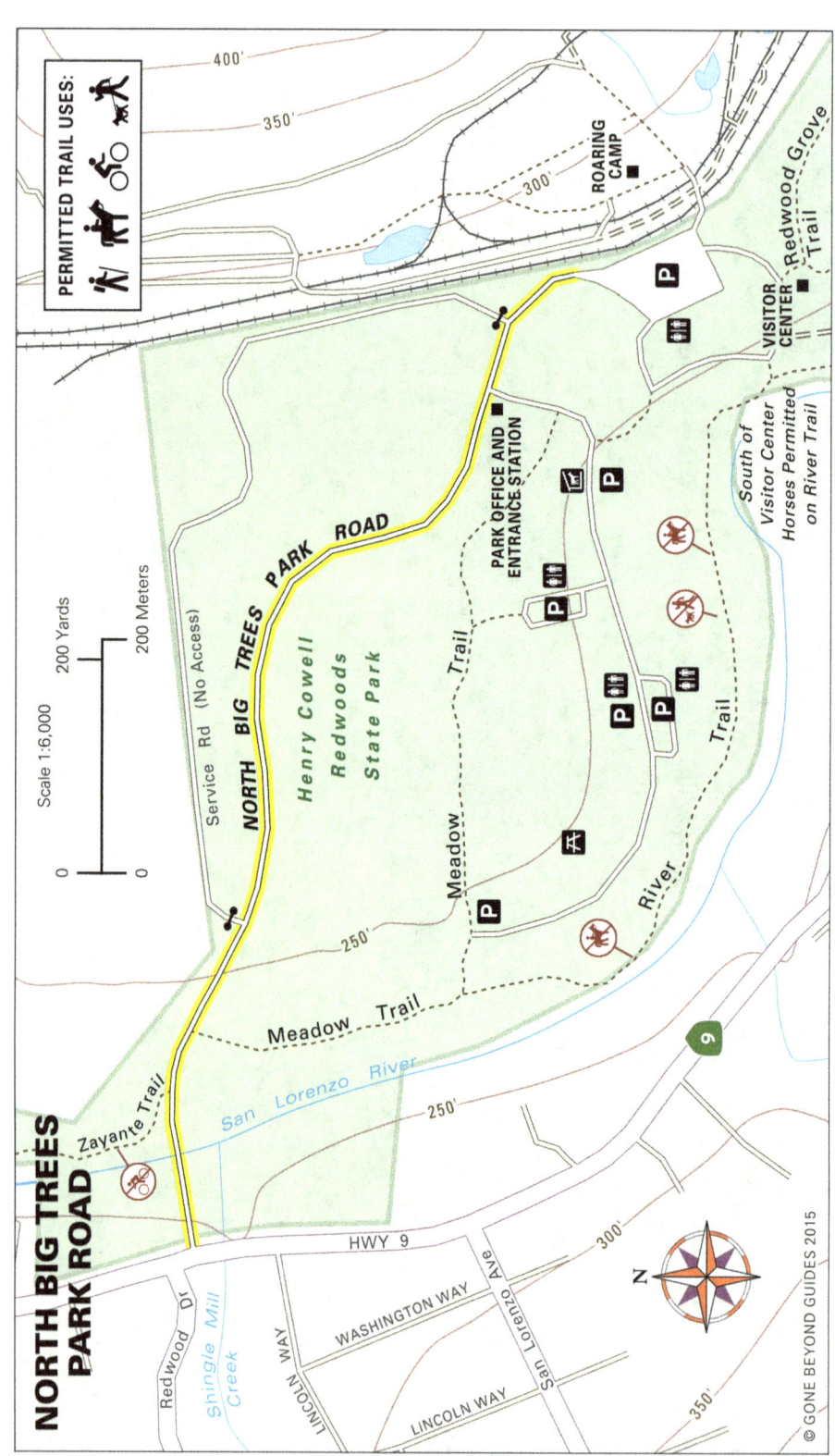

LEGEND

▭	Freeway
▭	Primary Road
▭	Secondary Road
▭	Unpaved Road
+++	Railroad
- - -	Featured Trail
- - -	Trail
▭	River / Stream
800'	Contour Line (intervals in feet)
♿	Accessible Feature
▲	Campground
⚲	Gate
🐴	Horse Staging Area
P	Parking
🧺	Picnic Area
🚻	Restrooms
🏠	Lookout
🚳	Bicycles Not Permitted
🐕‍🦺	Dogs Not Permitted
🐎	Horses Not Permitted
🅿	No Parking
🚴	Bicycles Permitted
🐕	Dogs on Leash Permitted
🚶	Hiking Permitted
🐴	Horses Permitted

Trails around the Entrance and Main Parking

North Big Trees Park Road

Difficulty: Easy

Distance: 0.7 miles / 1.1 km

Duration: 15 -30 minutes

Elevation Gain: Level

Best For: Getting from the Park's Entrance to the main parking lot

Okay, you can't exactly call something the "Complete" guide without covering every access road and trail. The North Big Trees Park Road is simply the entrance road to the main and overflow parking areas. Along it is the Park's Entrance Station where the day use fee is paid by the always friendly staff. Once paid, the road leads to the main parking and access to the Nature Store, Visitor Center, Redwood Grove Loop, the river beaches and restrooms.

Finding North Big Trees Road is done by heading out of Felton on Highway 9 towards Santa Cruz. Almost as soon as you are out of the town limits you will see a nice sign marking the entrance to the park on your left. The park's entrance does seem to greet the visitor, opening up nicely to the left with large redwoods surrounding a grassy meadow. Kids get a glimpse of the Roaring Camp Railroad in the distance, there is definitely a feeling you are about to create a life moment as the park unfolds before you.

For folks coming in from the parking just outside the park, the majority cut right onto the Meadow Trail and overflow parking roads to access the park rather than the main road. This route is shorter and avoids the awkward hugging of the road's shoulder as cars pass.

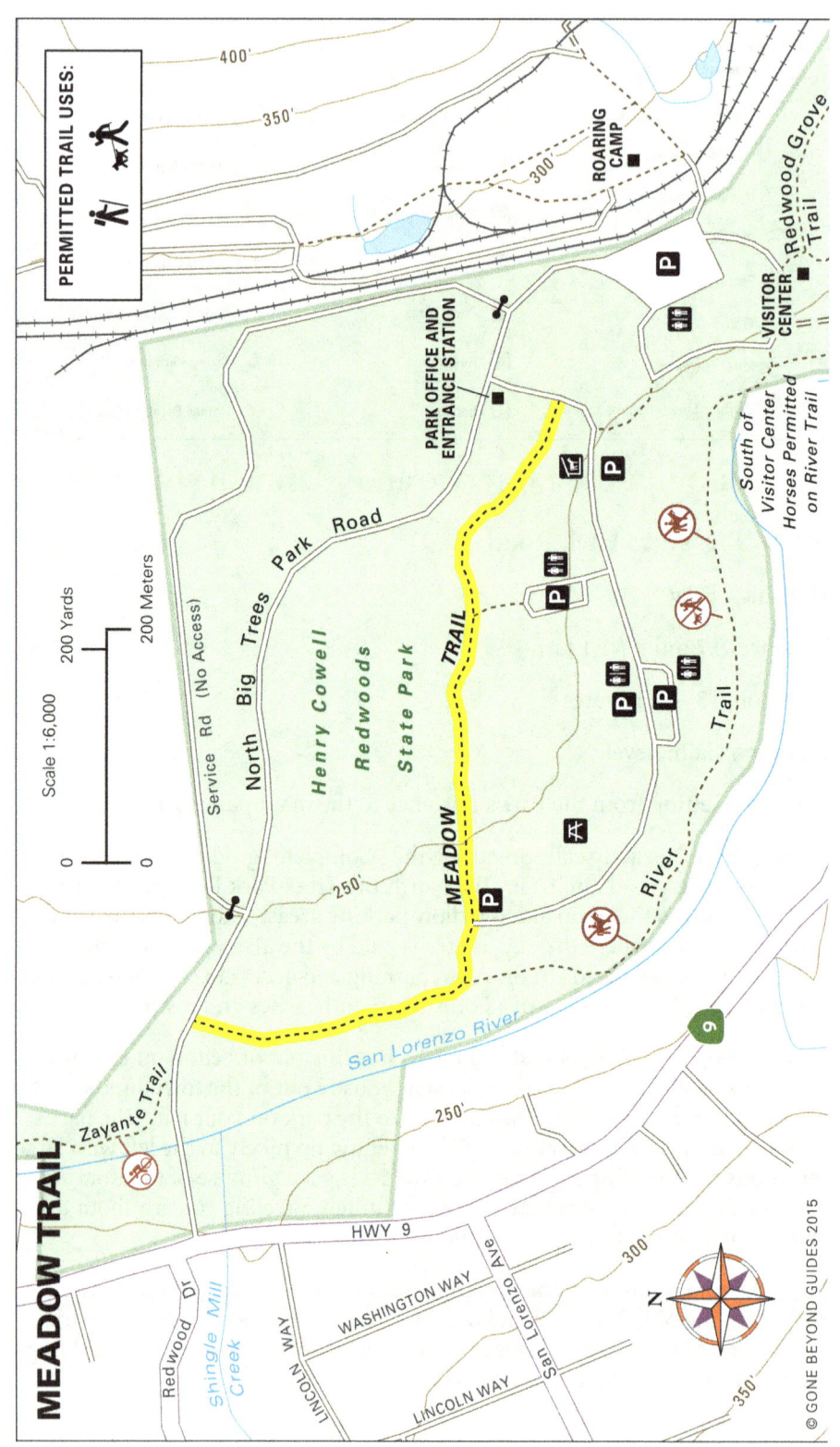

Meadow Trail

Difficulty: Easy

Distance: 0.6 miles / 1.0 km

Duration: 10 -15 minutes

Elevation Gain: Level

Best For: Rediscovering that you love the outdoors

The Meadow Trail is a casual little path that provides fairly quick access to the park's Visitor Center and Nature Store from Highway 9. Pick up the trail from the park's entrance just past the North Big Trees Road Bridge on your right. Meadow Trail ultimately ends at the main parking lot, connecting to the River Trail. For those that are just looking to get to the Visitor Center quickly can use the overflow parking access road, seen along this walk, as a shortcut.

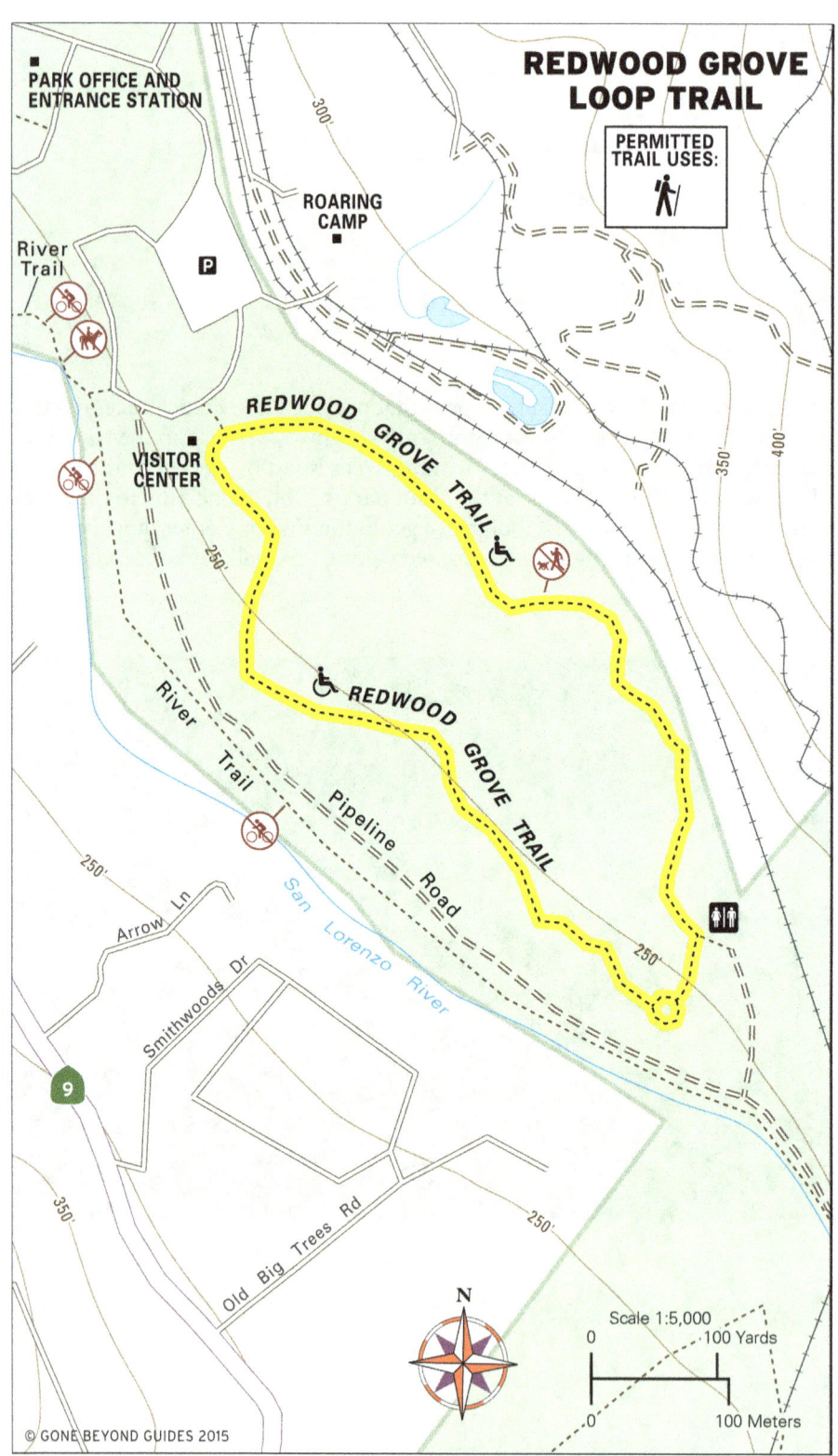

Redwood Grove Loop Trail

Difficulty: Easy

Distance: 0.8 miles / 1.3 km

Duration: 0.5-1 hour

Elevation Gain: Level

Best For: Families, quiet strolls, writing prose on majesty and wonder

The Redwood Grove Loop Trail is truly the gem of the park. One who walks this trail will experience the majesty and peace of walking amongst the almost sacred old growth Coastal Redwood (*Sequoia sempervirens*). The Coastal Redwood is officially the tallest tree in the world and is also amongst the largest. The tallest known redwood was measured at 379 feet. In comparison the Statue of Liberty is 305 feet from its foundation to its torch. The largest Coastal Redwood found in diameter is 26 feet, which is roughly the length of a small RV. The Coastal Redwood is also one of the longest lived plants, living more than 2000 years.

The Loop was once part of Welch's Big Trees Grove which is detailed in the Area History section. There are park interpretive guide brochures located at the beginning of the trail to allow the visitor a deeper immersion into the Redwood ecosystem. Besides seeing old growth coastal redwoods, the guide will also point the viewer to the non-native Dawn Redwood and a rare albino redwood. You can ask at the visitor center if you are interested in finding these.

The Redwood Grove Loop Trail is located at the end of the main visitor parking lot. The entire loop is designated as handicap accessible.

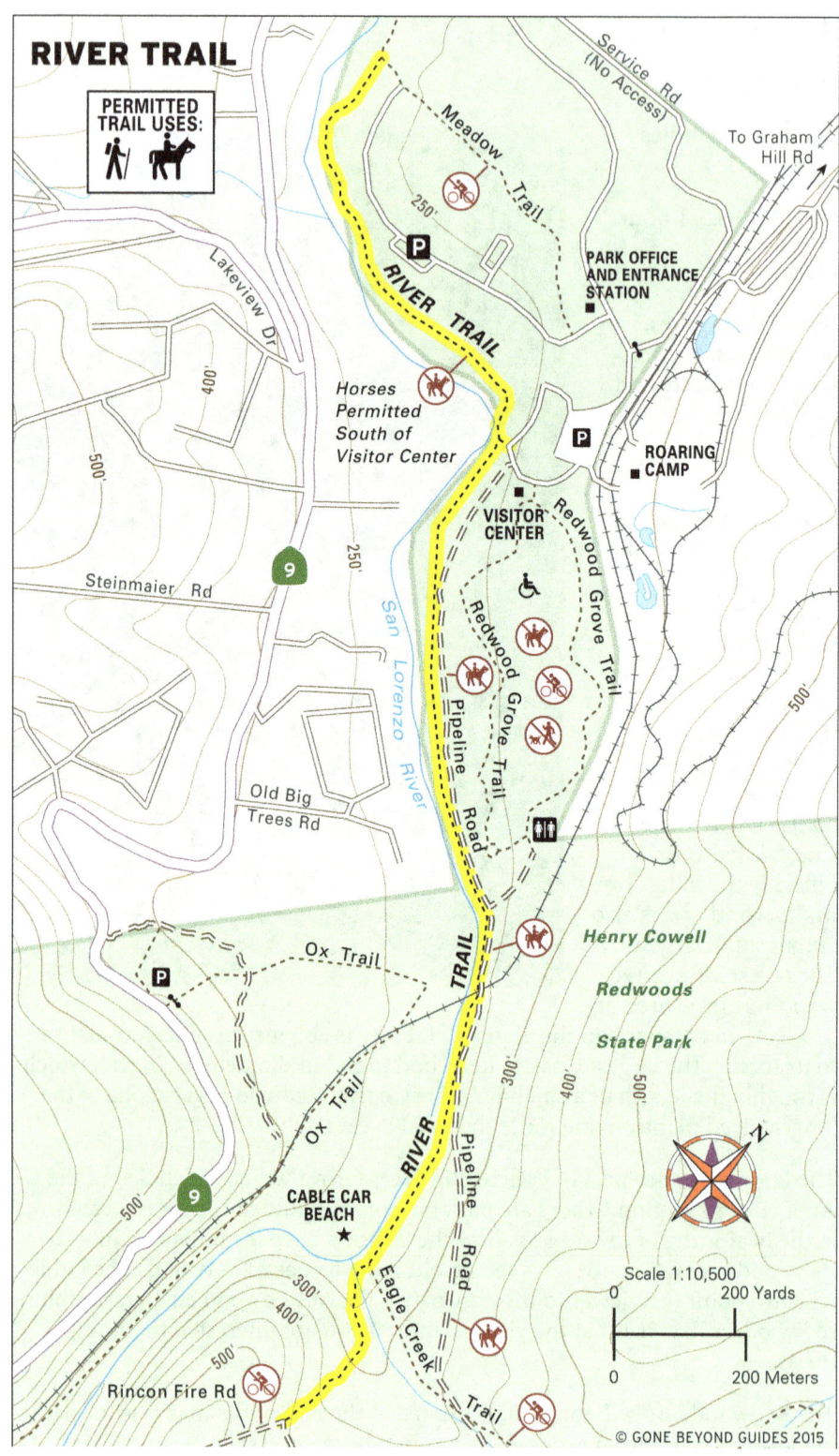

River Trail

Difficulty: Easy along river, moderately steep after leaving river

Distance: 1.7 miles / 2.7 km

Duration: 1 -1.5 hours

Elevation Gain/Loss: Level along river, 250 feet gain towards Rincon Fire Rd.

Best For: River beach goers, families and causal hikers

The River Trail winds along the San Lorenzo River from the Visitor Center to Cable Car Beach. From there it becomes a true single track as it climbs steeply to connect to the Rincon Fire Road. The trail does wind through itself with multiple tracks to choose from in some places. That being said, it is difficult for one to get lost on the trail, most of these offshoots are a reflection of the popularity of this trail as access to the many beaches along its path. The easy access of this trail makes it popular for families with small children.

Cable Car Beach is a popular strip of sand that becomes exposed in the summer months about one mile from the Visitor Center. This beach is very popular, especially with families. Downstream from the beach the river enters into a steep canyon that is fun to explore if you are looking for riverside adventure.

The River Trail never does cross the San Lorenzo River but does cross Eagle Creek. Once you cross, the trail heads steeply up to an unmarked intersection. Taking the left fork will put you quickly onto Rincon Fire Road. The right fork will do the same but is a bit longer.

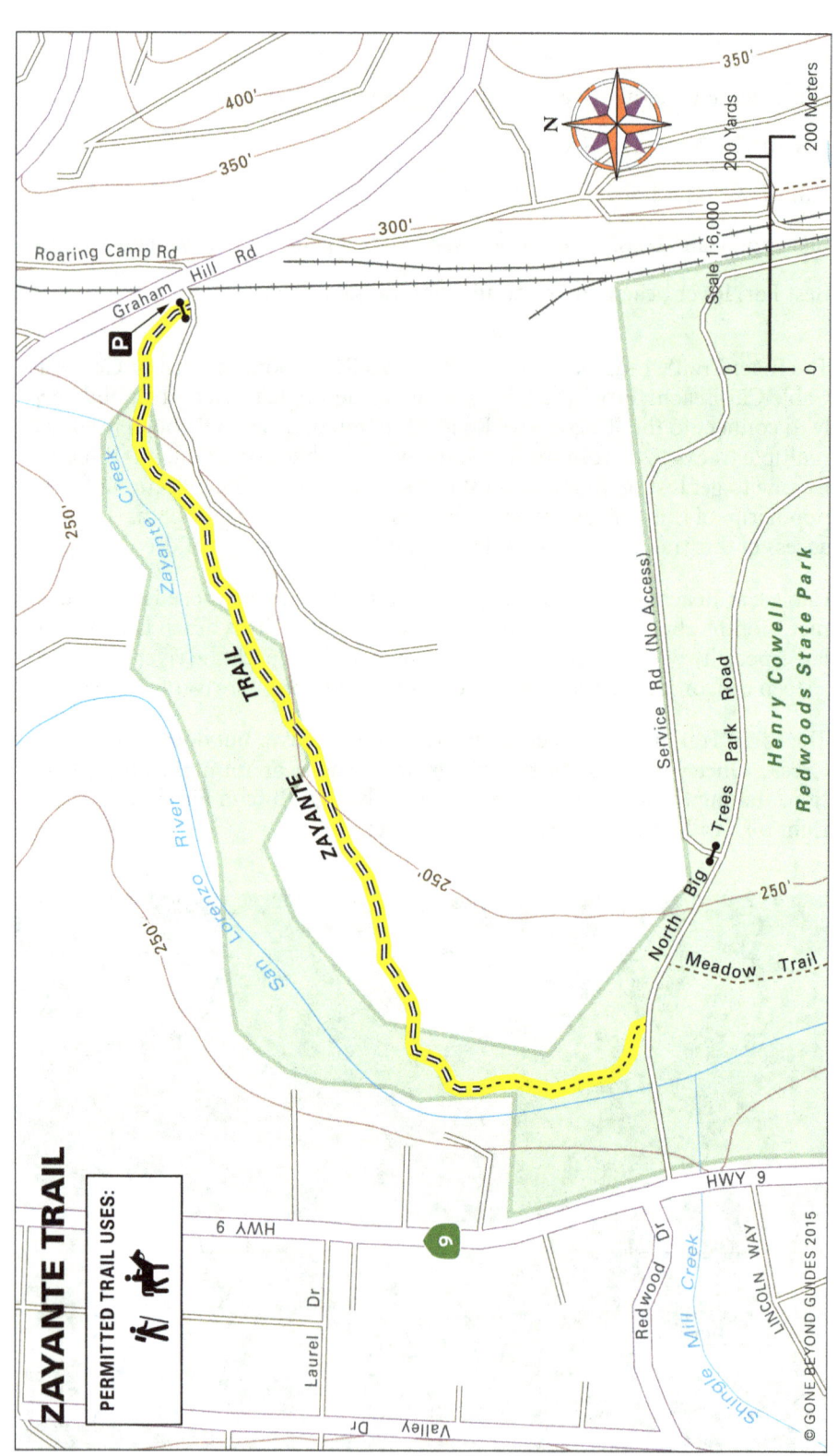

Zayante Trail

Difficulty: Easy

Distance: 0.6 miles / 1.0 km

Duration: 0.5 -1 hour

Elevation Gain/Loss: 30 feet

Best For: Getting a "local style" access to the park from the Felton Safeway.

Zayante Trail starts just south of Zayante Road in Felton on Graham Hill Road just past the Zayante Creek Bridge. If coming from Felton the trail is on your right. The trail is unmarked and closest public parking is either just up Graham Hill Road at a small pullout or 0.3 miles in town at the local Safeway. This trail contains some of the largest California sycamores and black cottonwoods found in the park.

The trail follows Zayante Creek and offers a nice back door entrance from the town of Felton straight into the park. After 1.1 miles Zayante Trail hooks into Meadow Trail.

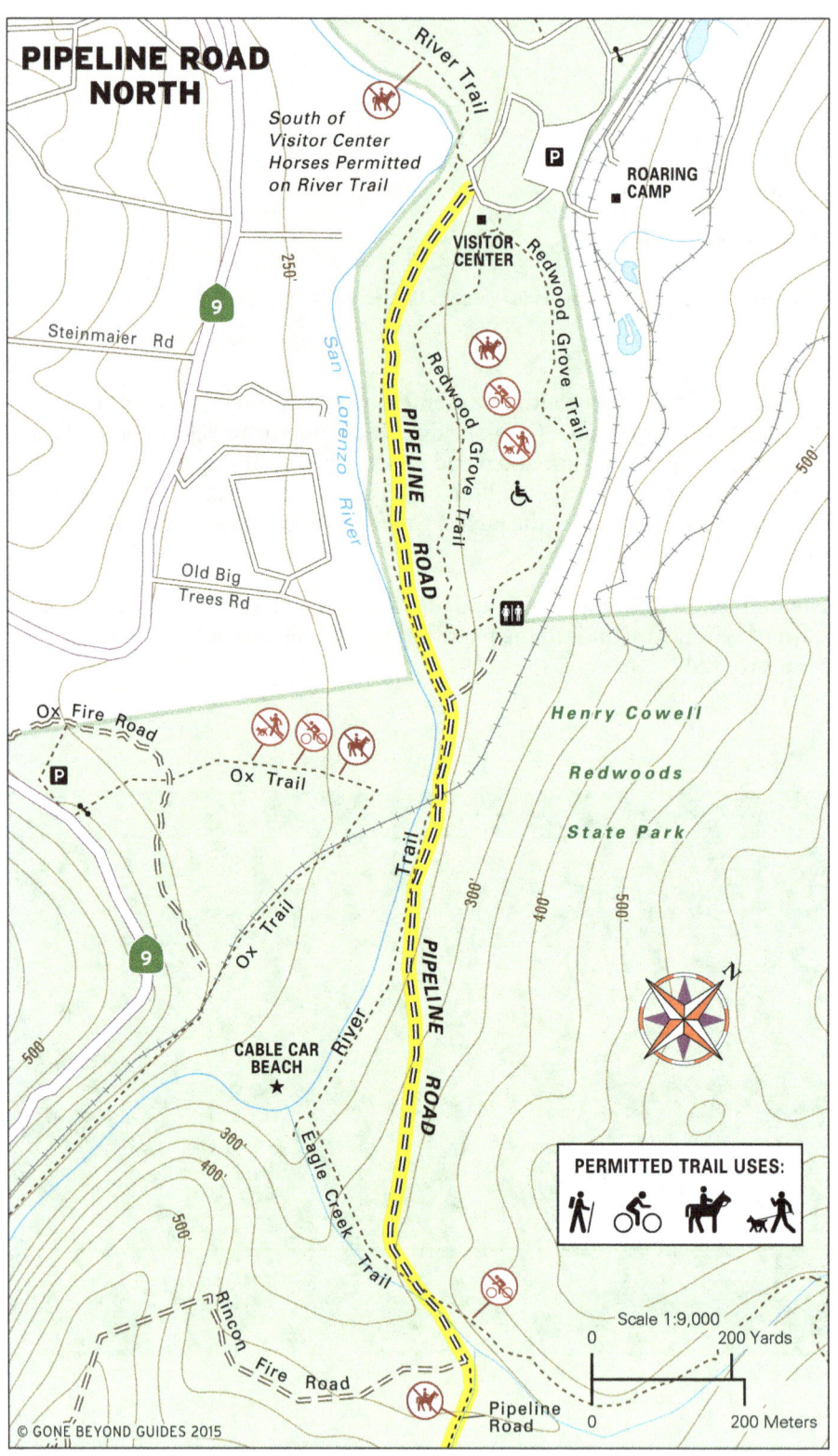

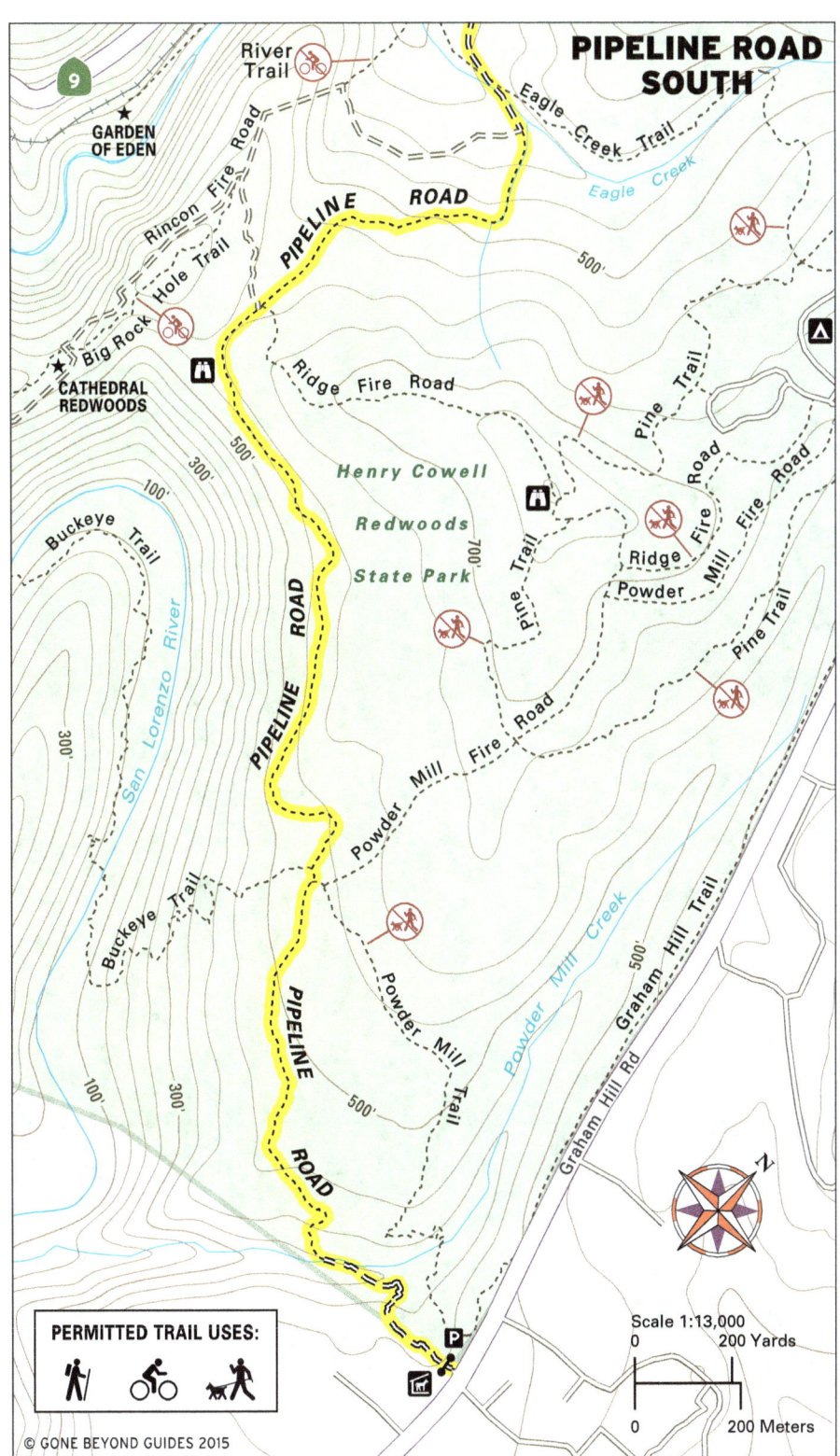

Pipeline Road

Difficulty: Easy along river, steep in sections after leaving the river

Distance: 3.3 miles / 5.3 km

Duration: 1-2 hours

Elevation Gain/Loss: 250 feet, very steep towards Graham Hill Road

Best For: Families and conversational hiking for the creek side sections, hill enthusiasts deeper in.

Pipeline Road starts shortly after the entrance of the park, meanders along the San Lorenzo River and then starts to climb up and down finally depositing the visitor at Graham Hill Road on the other side of the park. If you are looking for a representative cross section of the park, this is the trail for you.

One nice feature of this trail is that it is fully paved for its entire length. While it does get steep both up and down, this trail is fantastic for folks that want to get out but have trouble with uneven surfaces. As the trail is allowed for mountain biking, Pipeline Road can also be a great "first trail", though you will need those granny gears as you leave the river.

Pipeline Road can be picked up behind the Visitor Center. The first leg of the trail is flat with great views of the San Lorenzo River. The trail crosses under a train trestle and begins to climb. The climb is moderately steep bringing some relief after about a half mile. The trail will encounter some steeper downhill sections at this point; level off for a bit before making one final steep climb to end at Graham Hill Road. This final part contains a whopping 38% grade, but fortunately isn't terribly long. The Overlook Bench is a great place to relax. Dogs are allowed on Pipeline Road as are horses up to Rincon Fire Road.

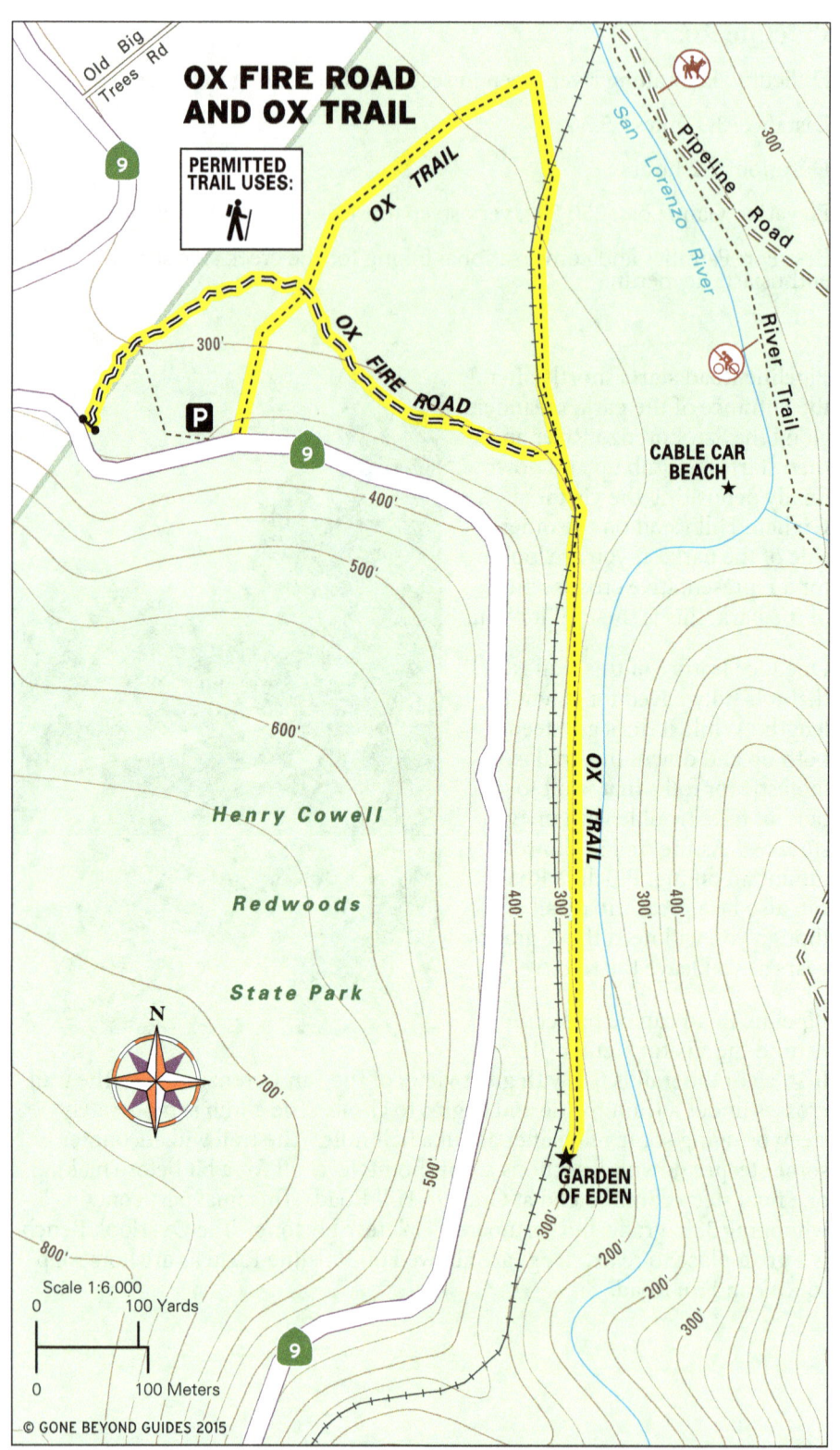

Trails Closer to the San Lorenzo River (West Half)

Ox Fire Road/Ox Trail

Difficulty: Easy with short steep pitch to river

Distance: 0.7 miles / 1.3 km

Duration: 0.5-1 hour

Elevation Gain/Loss: 100 feet, steeper towards river

Best For: Beach Babylon river style

The officially named Ox Fire Road is known more commonly as the Ox Trail. This trail is well known amongst the locals and is principally used to access Garden of Eden Beach. Marked parking for the trail is about 1.2 miles from the entrance of Henry Cowell on Highway 9 towards Santa Cruz.

The trail connects and follows parallel with the railroad tracks after the first half mile. There is a marked sign for Garden of Eden beach. Cross the tracks and head down the final leg to the beach. Garden of Eden beach is a great place to cool off during the summer. The short hike in finding the beach will reward the visitor with two deep swimming holes amongst some large river rocks and a small spit of sand. In spite of it being a bit of a journey to get to this beach, it is well-known and can get crowded.

There are some unmarked spur trails just after crossing the railroad tracks, one of which will bring the user to a wide sandy beach and potentially greater solitude. Look for the "State Property" sign on a tall tree stump to indicate you are on the right unmarked trail. Whatever you do, do not take any one of the other unmarked spur trails. These do not lead to even more spectacular beaches but are rumored to all end at an evil witch's house that is made entirely out of gingerbread. If your name is Hansel or Gretel, be especially cautious as the end result can be quite grim. Of course, this warning could simply be the author's way of reducing unofficial trail usage within the park.

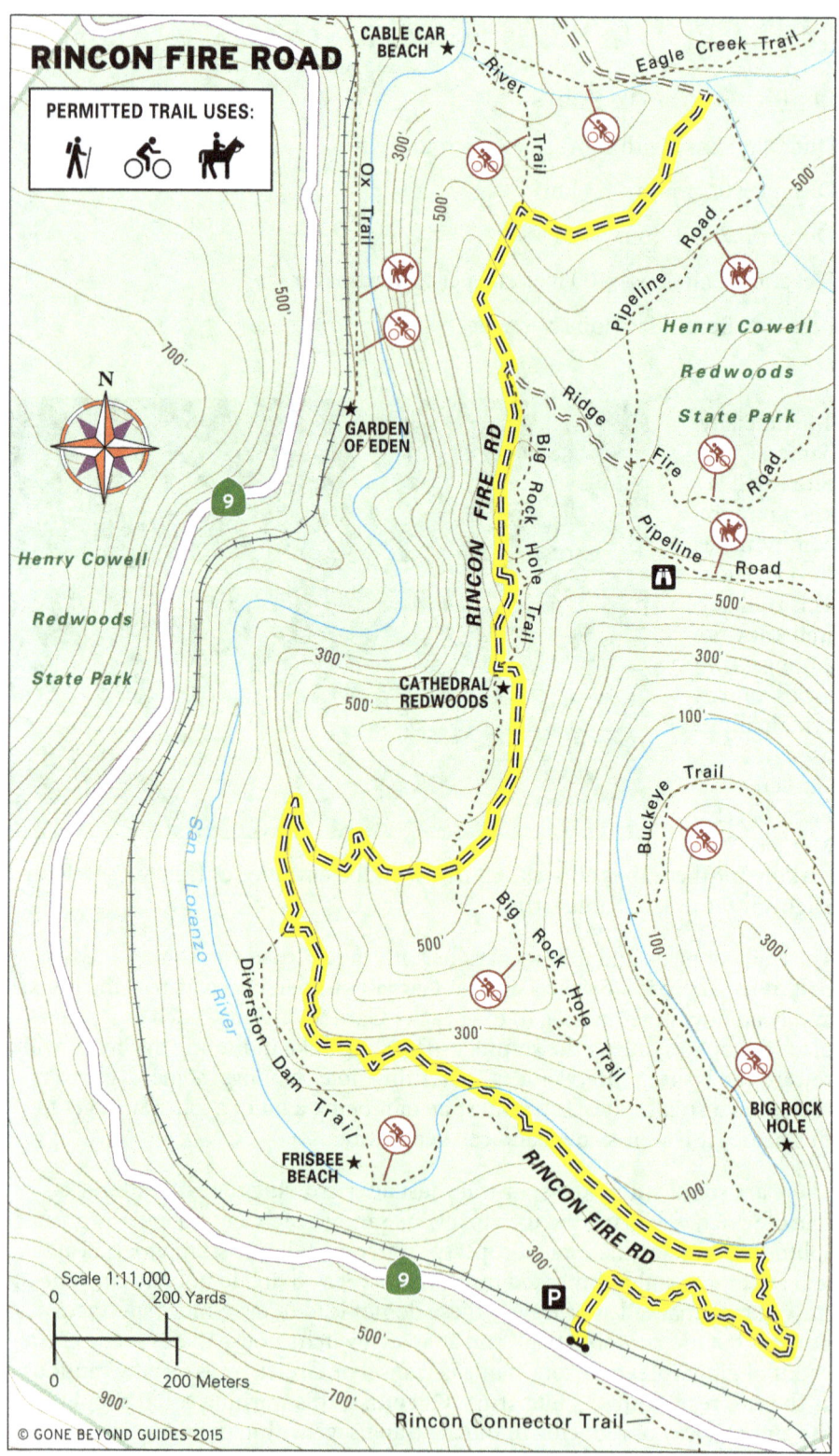

Rincon Fire Road

Difficulty: Steep in sections, one river crossing

Distance: 2.6 miles / 4.2 km

Duration: 1-3 hours

Elevation Gain/Loss: 275 feet

Best For: Taking in a good cross section of the park

Rincon Fire Road can be accessed from Pipeline Road or a little farther down via River Road. Rincon offers a nice cut of the park, giving a little of everything the main unit offers aside from the sandy loam sections. It can also be combined for some lengthier loops.

Starting at Pipeline Road the trail starts out moderately and continues to climb past the connection to River Trail and the connection to the start of Big Rock Hole Trail. From this point to the first Big Rock Hole intersection, the trail goes down through redwoods and then heads steeply down on the other side of the ridge. There is a nice glimpse of the far mountains across the San Lorenzo River at one point.

From here the trail goes fairly steeply downhill amongst mixed evergreen, Douglas fir and some redwoods. The final leg from Diversion Dam to the river makes an unexpected uphill climb before dropping steeply and quickly to the river bank. The trail is often covered with bay and redwood leaves mixed with loose gravel so watch your step.

Once at the river, crossing is fairly straight forward in the summer, deeper and wetter in the winter. The area can receive tremendous volumes of rain and there are times when the river is dangerous to cross, use caution. There are some pleasant rapids upstream of the crossing. Once you cross, the road will follow the river downstream for about a half mile or so before climbing up to Highway 9 and the Rincon Parking lot. There are several short cut trails along this section though these are officially off limits. Rincon Parking lot is 3.2 miles from the main entrance of Henry Cowell heading south towards Santa Cruz on Highway 9.

Right before the trail heads to the parking lot, look for the junction for Buckeye and Big Rock Hole Trails. Just before Big Rock Swimming Hole are the remains of a 1300 foot flume that diverted water to the California Powder Works, a gunpowder manufacturing facility that operated in the late 1800's.

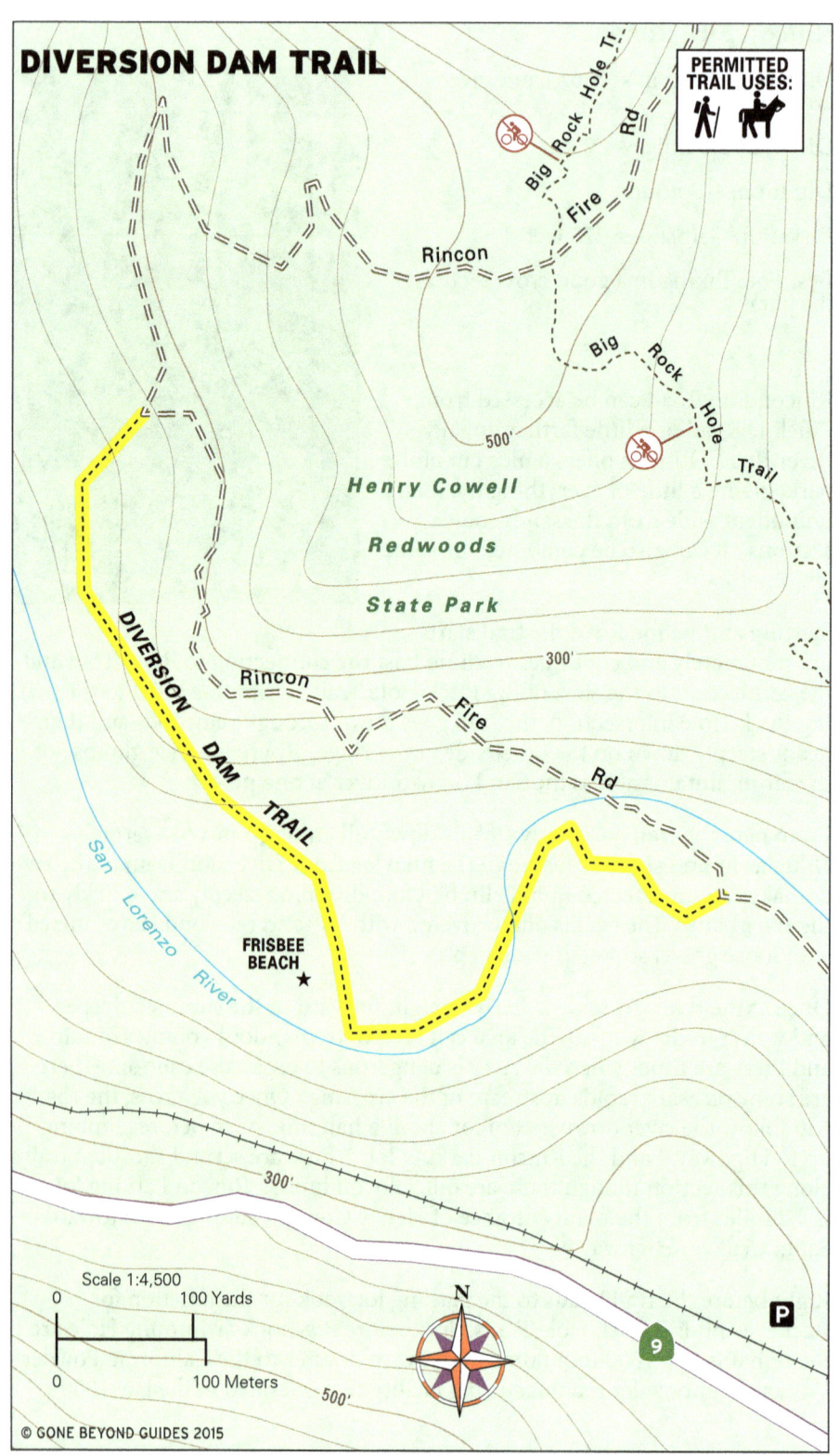

Diversion Dam Trail

Difficulty: Steep in sections, river crossing

Distance: 0.7 miles / 1.1 km

Duration: 0.5 -1 hour

Elevation Gain:/Loss 100 feet

Best For: Getting to Frisbee Beach

Diversion Dam trailhead begins from the Rincon Fire Road parking lot and is well-marked. Take the Rincon Fire Road on the right side of the parking lot straight down to the river's side and continue upstream until meeting up with the Diversion Dam Trail.

The trail on this side of the river heads up into the hills and then back down. At the top of the trail is a nice view of the old Diversion Dam, which was once used to divert water for the gunpowder manufacturing company called the California Powder Works. Water would build up in the dam and be diverted via a flume that went 1200 feet through the mountain to the Powder Works facility. In the summer, the whole of the San Lorenzo River would be diverted. The tunnel has since collapsed and only trace remnants remain of the flumes.

Once the trail reaches back down to the river, the crossing is just below a set of rapids above the dam. The trail on both sides of the river does tend to get overgrown and is not well-marked, especially in the winter. You will know you are at the crossing by the obvious path down to the river's banks. The trail does continue upstream and looks like the official trail for about 100 yards before narrowing into an unofficial creek side trail. Frisbee Beach is just above the rapids on the other side of the river. Frisbee Beach offers a nice swimming hole and some sandy beach for visitors to enjoy.

Once on the other side, the trail is rutted, uneven and steep as it ascends the canyon back up to Rincon Fire Road.

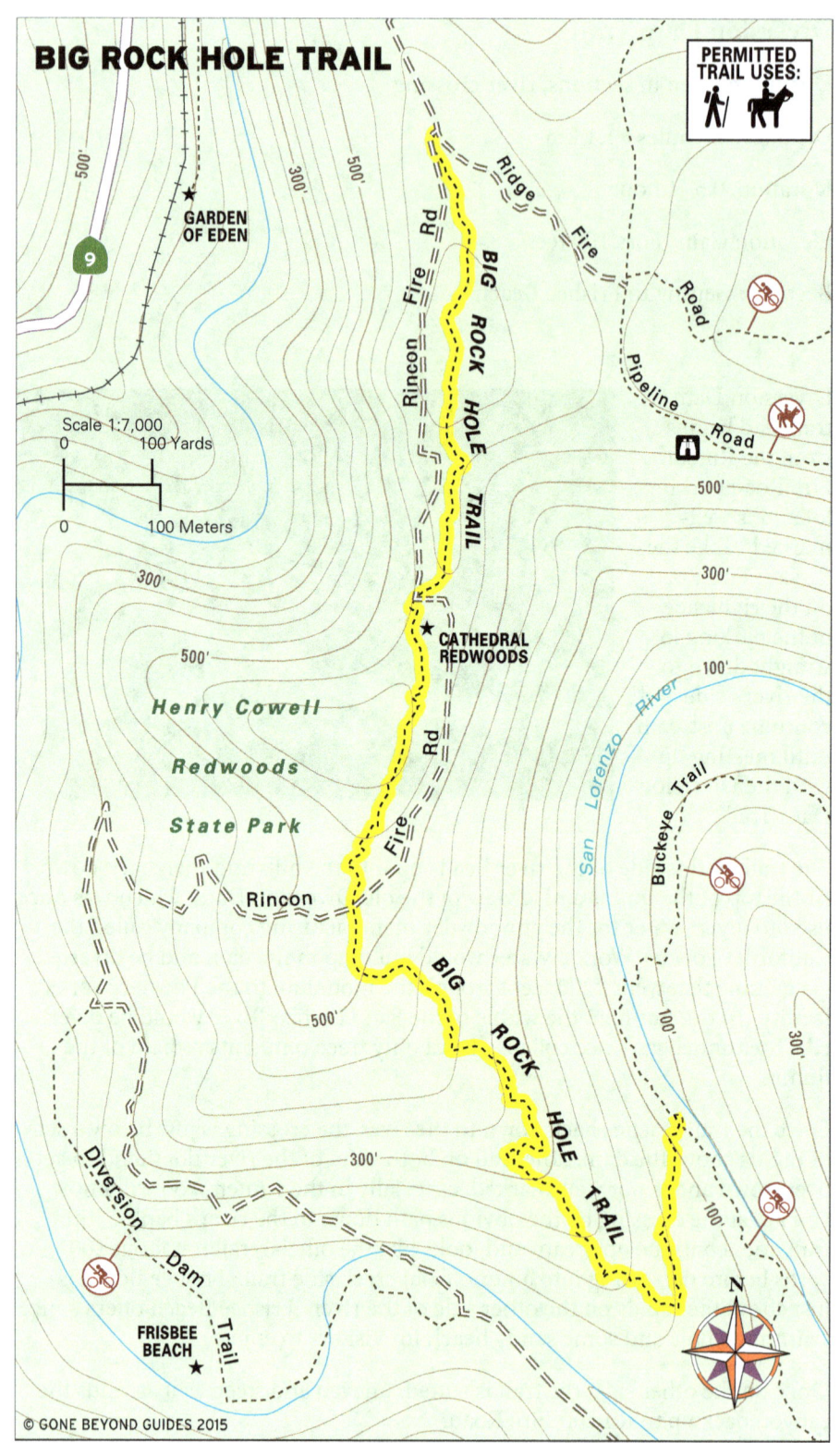

Big Rock Hole Trail

Difficulty: Moderate, steep in sections

Distance: 0.9 miles / 1.4 km

Duration: 0.5-1 hour

Elevation Gain / Loss: 400 feet

Best For: Finding a small grove of old growth redwoods and a rope swing

You can pick up Big Rock Hole Trail from either the end closer to the visitor center or from the San Lorenzo River. Since getting to the river is straightforward, we will describe the trail starting from the end closer to the visitor center. Big Rock Hole Trail starts at the well-marked four way intersection that also includes Ridge Fire Road and Rincon Fire Road. This section of the trail runs essentially parallel to the Rincon Fire Road but offers a more intimate single track hiking alternative to the wider Rincon Fire Road. The first section is a mixture of redwoods and evergreens and holds a fairly easy grade for this section.

Immediately after crossing Rincon Fire Road the first time you will find Cathedral Redwoods on your left. This area is a very pleasant spot to relax and take a break. Large old growth benches have been cut to sit on all of which are encircled by fairly mature redwoods. One patch of this cathedral has endured a fire at one point and displays a nice example of the tenacity of the redwood to thrive in spite of fire.

The section from the first crossing of Rincon is almost entirely second growth redwoods with the occasional old growth tree that was too gnarled to cut down. Once it crosses Rincon Fire Road the second time the trail climbs for a very short bit to the top of a small hill and then heads steadily and at times steeply down to the Big Rock (Swimming) Hole. Many folks see the trail name and look for a big rock with a hole in it. In fact, the name is given to a swimming hole next to a big rock. This of course is not as exciting as finding a big rock with a hole in it but it is a popular swimming hole all the same. The swimming hole from this direction will require two river crossings as the river splits to form an island. The hole is on the other side of the farthest downstream section of the island. Big Rock Hole Trail ends at the swimming hole, connecting to Rincon Fire Road and the Rincon Parking Lot.

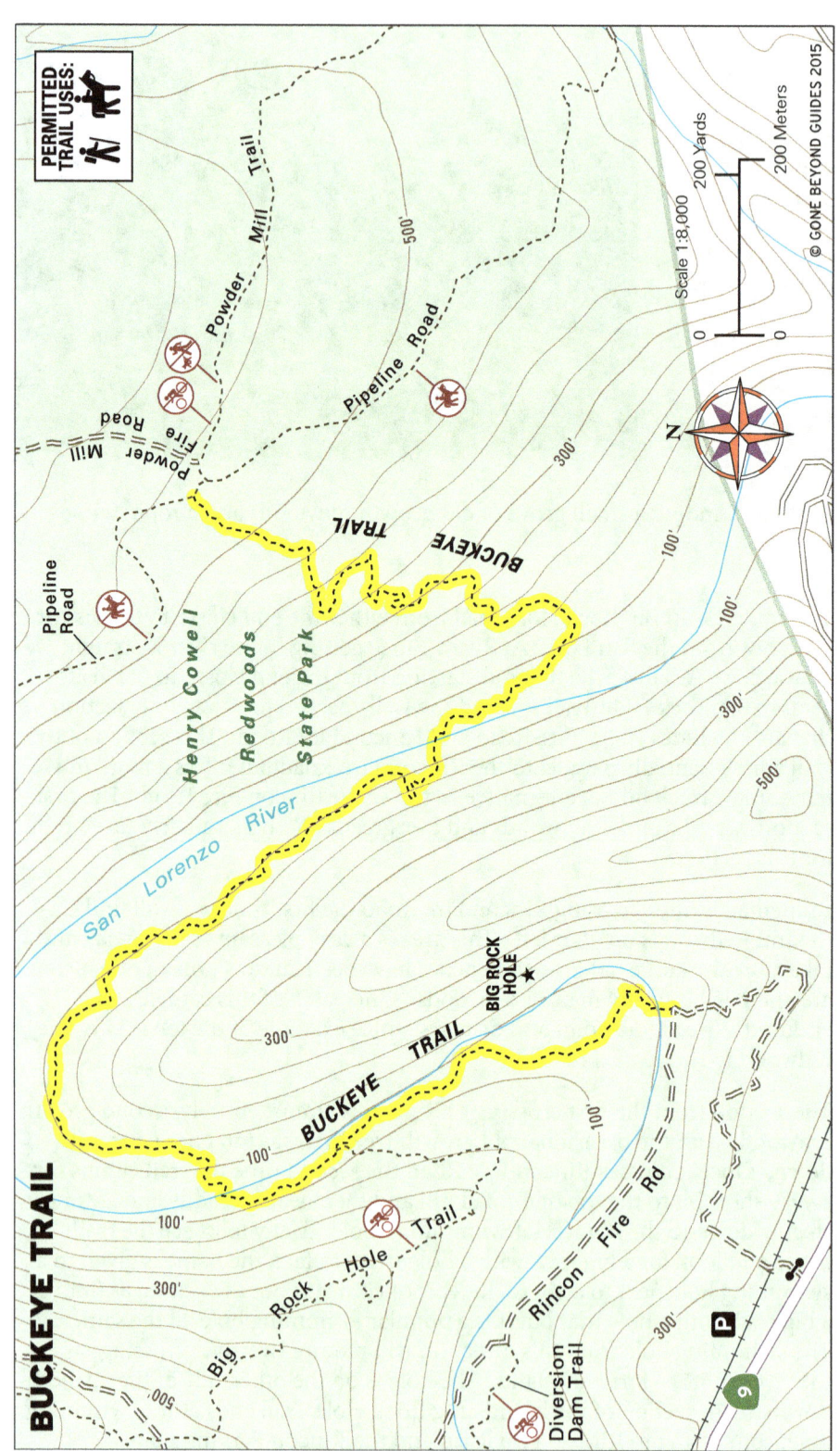

Buckeye Trail

Difficulty: Moderate with some steep sections, river crossings

Distance: 1.6 miles / 2.6 km

Duration: 1-3 hours

Elevation Gain/Loss: 400 feet

Best For: Feeling consumed by the wilderness, inspiration, and resetting

Buckeye Trail is close to perfect for those looking for a true wilderness hike. The trail crosses the San Lorenzo River officially four times and rests alongside it for much of the hike. This section of the river passes through a forested canyon giving the visitor a sense of isolation and adventure.

To access the trail park at the Rincon Parking lot 3.2 miles from the main entrance along Highway 9 as it heads south to Santa Cruz. From almost the moment you hit the trail you will hear the sound of the San Lorenzo River, fearsome during a winter storm and gentle as the wind babbling through quacking aspens in the summer. From Rincon Fire Road head down to meet up with the river, crossing it once to get to a small island, again to get to the other side of the river and once again just after passing the junction to Big Rock Hole Trail. These three crossings are fairly easy to navigate, especially in the summer.

The trail follows the river at this point as it cuts a horseshoe bend around a steep ridge, however is relatively flat for the hiker.

The trail crosses the San Lorenzo once again and then steeply climbs up switchbacks through groves of redwood to the 5 way intersection of Pipeline and Powder Mill Trail. At the river crossing, the trail is up/down river about 100 feet depending on which direction you are travelling.

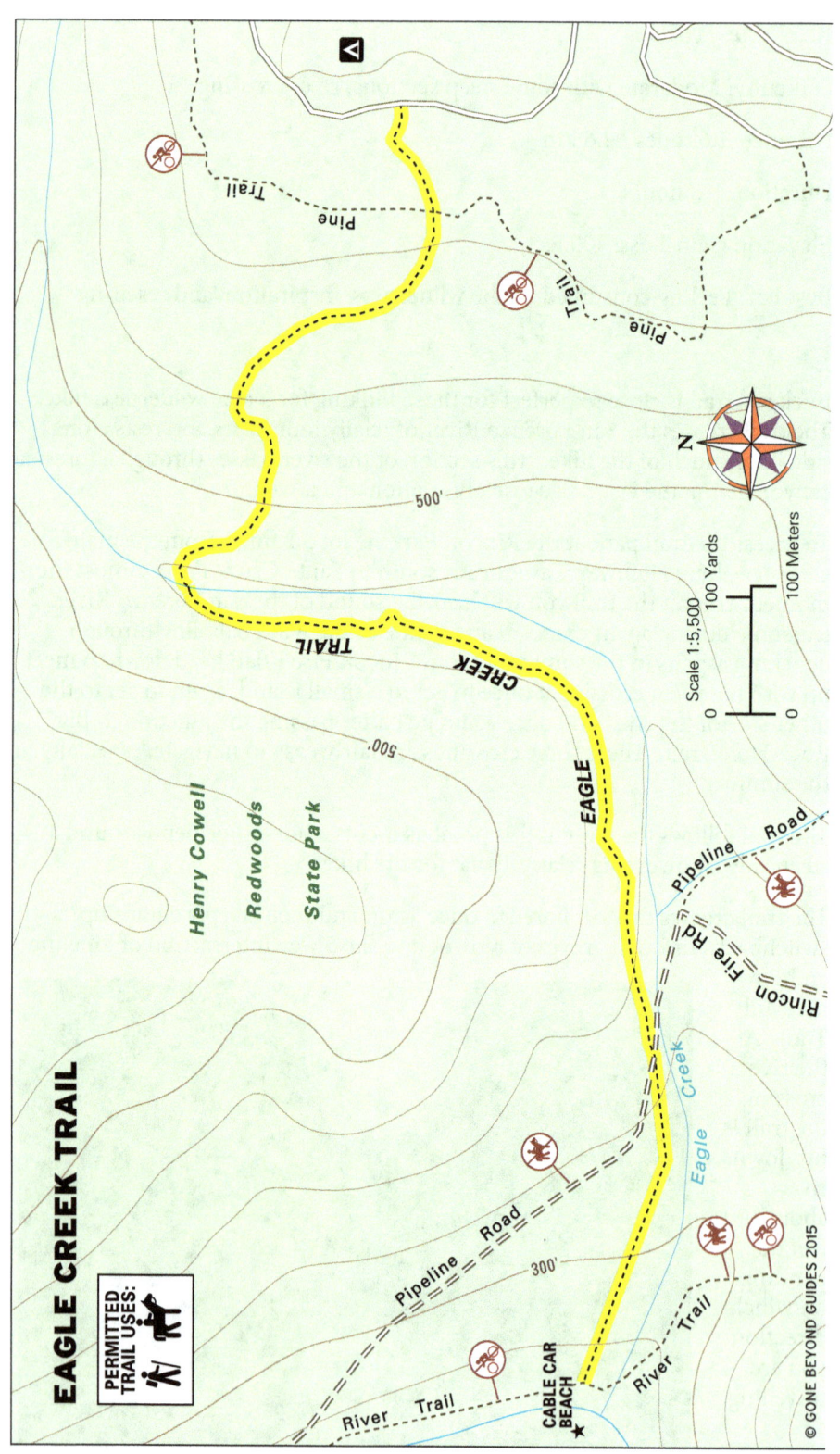

Trails Closer to the Campground (East Half)

Eagle Creek Trail

Difficulty: Moderately steep

Distance: 0.9 miles / 1.4 km

Duration: 0.5 to 1 hours

Elevation Gain/Loss: 200 feet

Best For: Finding a romantic bridge tucked away in a forest of redwoods

Eagle Creek Trail can be picked up from the Henry Cowell Campground near Site #82. From the campground, the trail curves its way in a deliberate path pretty much straight down. The trail has a number of wide steps cut into some of the steeper sections. Eagle Creek will quickly unite the traveler with Pipeline Road and the river where the trail ends. Be prepared for a steep climb back if returning the same way. There is one old growth redwoods and burnt out old growth stumps along visible along the trail. There is also a quaint little bridge to cross Eagle Creek.

If you are coming in from the campground day use parking area, its useful to know the campground is split into two loops, take the right most one (the one with the higher numbered sites) and then keep left until you pick up the obvious countdown to site #82. This trail is okay for hikers and horses.

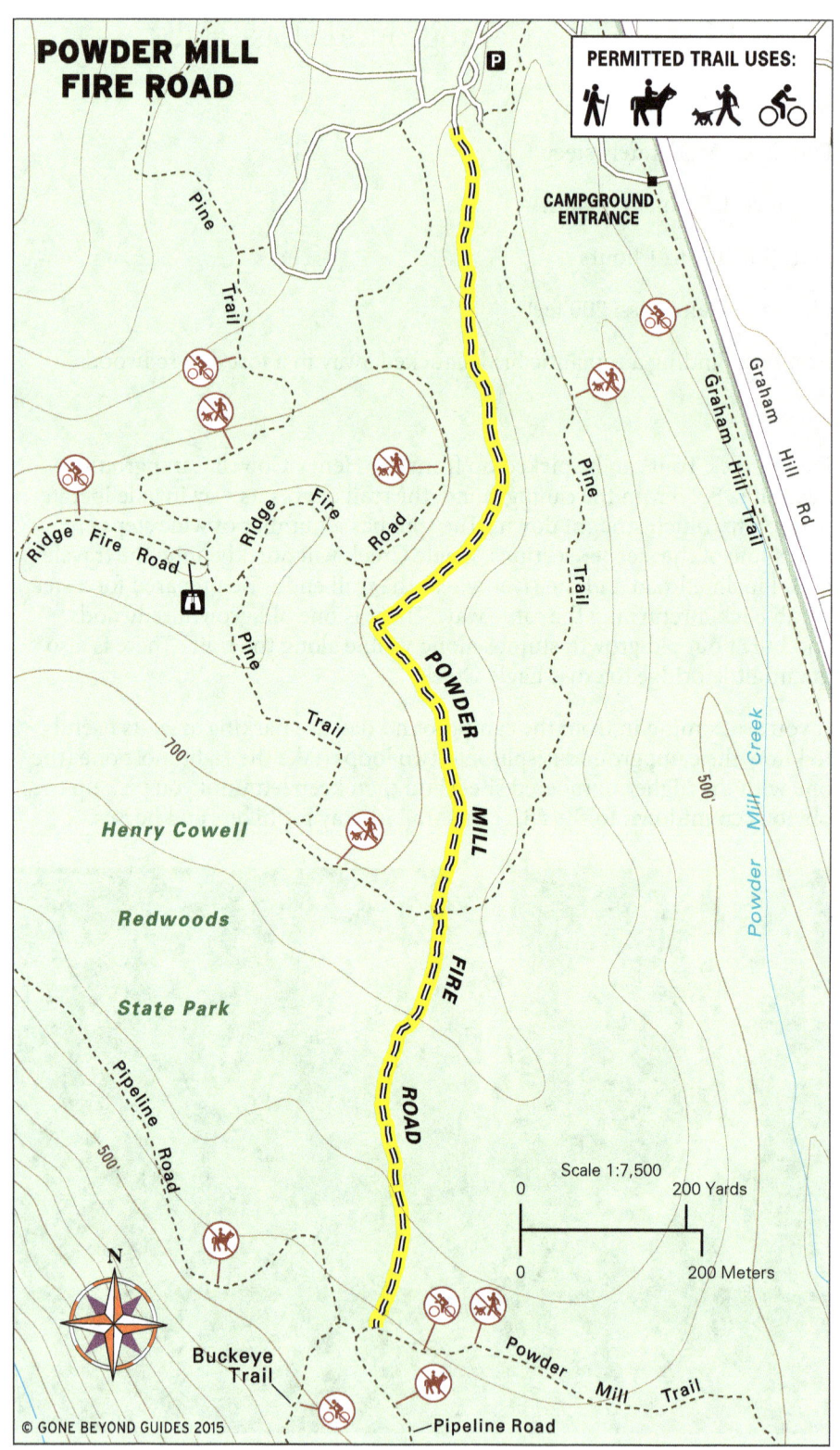

Powder Mill Fire Road

Difficulty: Moderate to Steep

Distance: 1.0 miles / 1.6 km

Duration: 1-2 hours

Elevation Gain/Loss: 200 feet

Best For: Getting from your campsite to a more secluded section of the river.

The Powder Mill Fire Road and the Powder Mill Trail are both named after the nearby California Powder Works, a gunpowder manufacturing facility in operation from 1861 to 1914. There is a more detailed section on the California Powder Works in the Area History section.

Powder Mill Fire Road is a wide trail that can be a little hilly at times, cutting through mixed evergreen forests. The trail ends at the five way junction of Powder Mill Trail, Pipeline Road and Buckeye Trail.

You can make a short detour to the Ridge Fire Road Observation Deck and is well worth the visit, giving 360 degree views as far as Monterey and to the north showing the vastness of the ancient Santa Cruz Sandhills.

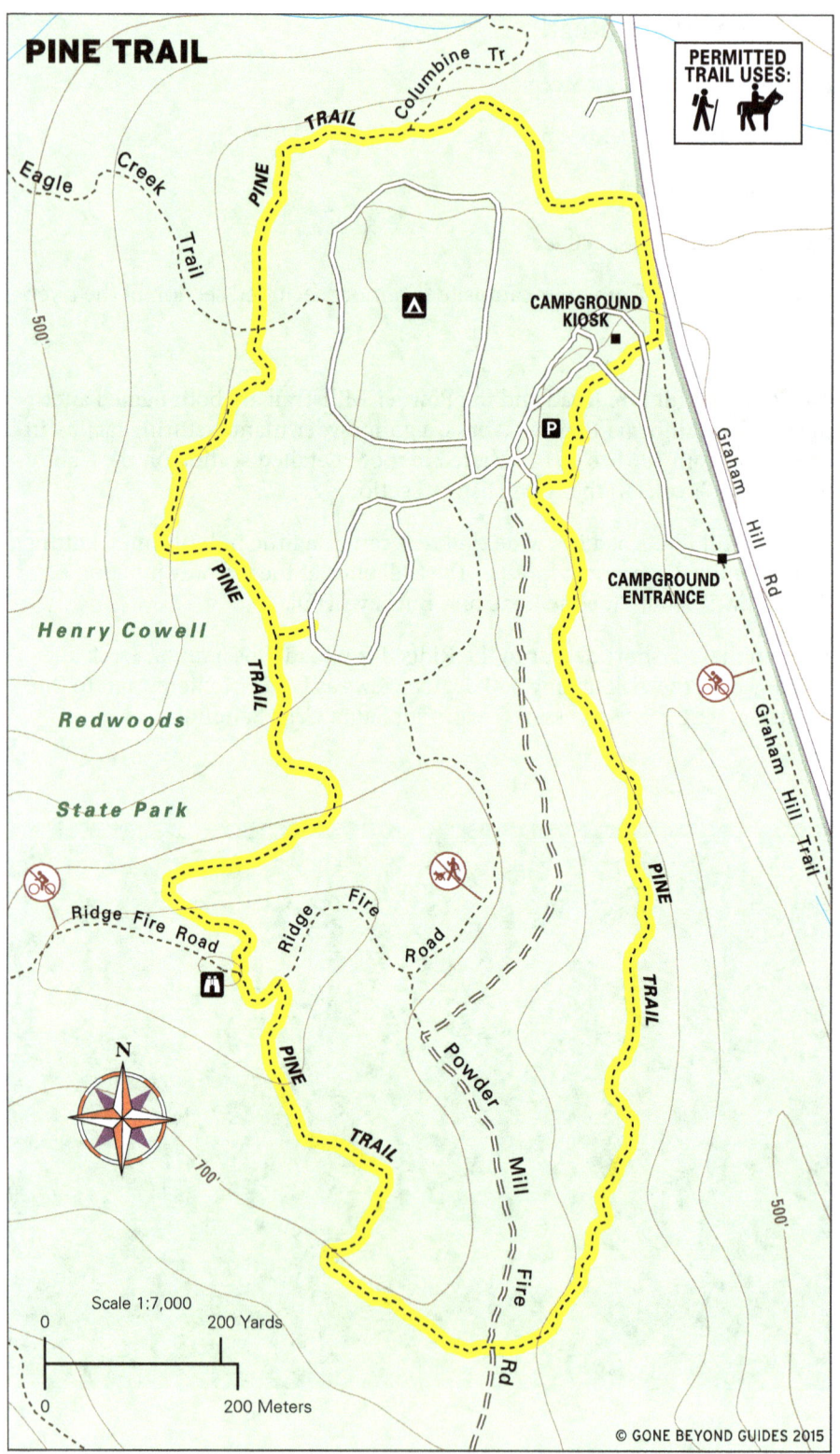

Pine Trail

Difficulty: Easy to moderate, very sandy in spots

Distance: 2.2 miles / 3.5 km

Duration: 1-3 hours

Elevation Gain/Loss: 175 feet

Best For: Families looking for a nice loop near their campsite

Pine Trail takes a broad loop around the Henry Cowell Campground, intersects nicely with a number of offshoot trails and even offers an observation tower with a 360 degree view. It can be downright sandy at times and visitors may wonder if they are hiking a sand dune, which in reality they are. Loose sand aside, Pine Trail does make for a nice loop for visitors camping in the park.

You can pick up the Pine Trail just to right of the Campfire Center/outdoor auditorium. The trail heads south to the Powder Mill Fire Road through a pleasant wooded area of mixed evergreens. Pine Trail continues through a wooded thicket until meeting up with the Ridge Fire Road Observation Deck. This deck gives very nice views as far south as Monterey and equally nice views to the north as well. The deck has a drinking fountain and a couple of nature signs describing the ancient sand dunes you are walking on.

The section following the observation tower is fairly flat, though a bit sandy. This area is a great example of the Santa Cruz Sandhills ecosystem. These sandhills were once part of the sea floor, now some 4 miles inland from the oceans current position. Over thousands of years, plants have taken hold, surviving in the sandy soil and eventually creating the unique forest in front of you.

Pine Trail crosses a junction early on that is unmarked but will lead to the campground at sites #48 and #49. Continuing will take you to the well-marked Eagle Creek Trail and eventually Columbine Trail. There is one additional trail back to the campgrounds just after Columbine. Staying on Pine Trail will put you onto the beginning of Graham Hill Trail for a short spell where you can pick up Pine once more just after the campground entrance.

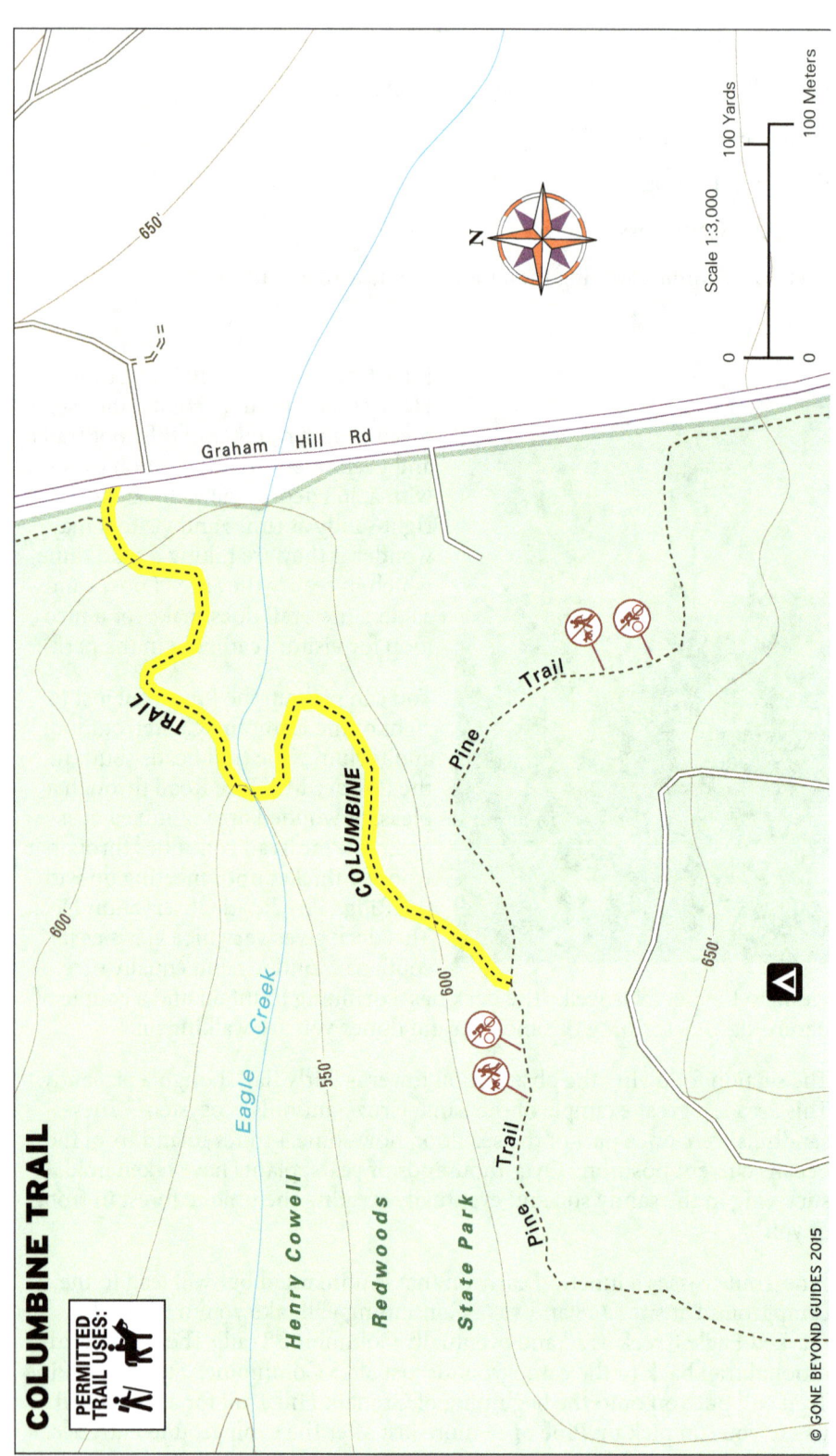

Columbine Trail

Difficulty: Easy to Moderate

Distance: 0.5 miles / 1.0 km

Duration: 0.5 -1 hour

Elevation Gain/Loss: 200 feet

Best For: Midnight dares

There are very few times that one gets an unsettled feeling just from hiking a trail, but if ever there was one that produces this feeling, the Columbine Trail is it. The trail is mossy, watery, and full of boggy fermenting smells. It is a place where one wonders what happened to make it feel so odd, it feels like bad things have happened here. Worse, it feels like aspects of whatever happened have never left and still wander in the area. Adding to this, parts of the trail are exposed with black ground tarps sticking out as if it is covering an ancient cemetery or perhaps something even worse. There is a quickness of step one takes when treading on this trail. You don't want to stop, you want it to stop and the only way for the creepy feeling to end is to just keep walking.

You can pick up Columbine Trail from Pine Trail near the northeast section of the campground near campsite #72. Continue down to the small overgrown creek where the creepy feelings begin. If you dare, stop for a moment and just stand still for a couple of minutes. The unexpected cracking of that branch, the unsettling slurping sound like leeches are crawling up your leg perhaps, the rustling of the brush behind you, is it all in your imagination? Oh dear reader, you wonder if the author is playing with your good senses, but that is not the case. Get up from your campsite and take your best flashlights to prove for yourself that this is true. There is something unnatural here, see for yourself. You will enter into a damp riparian area, especially in winter, muddy and mossy before climbing up briefly to exit at around 5000 Graham Hill Road. There is parking for at most two cars here if coming from this direction.

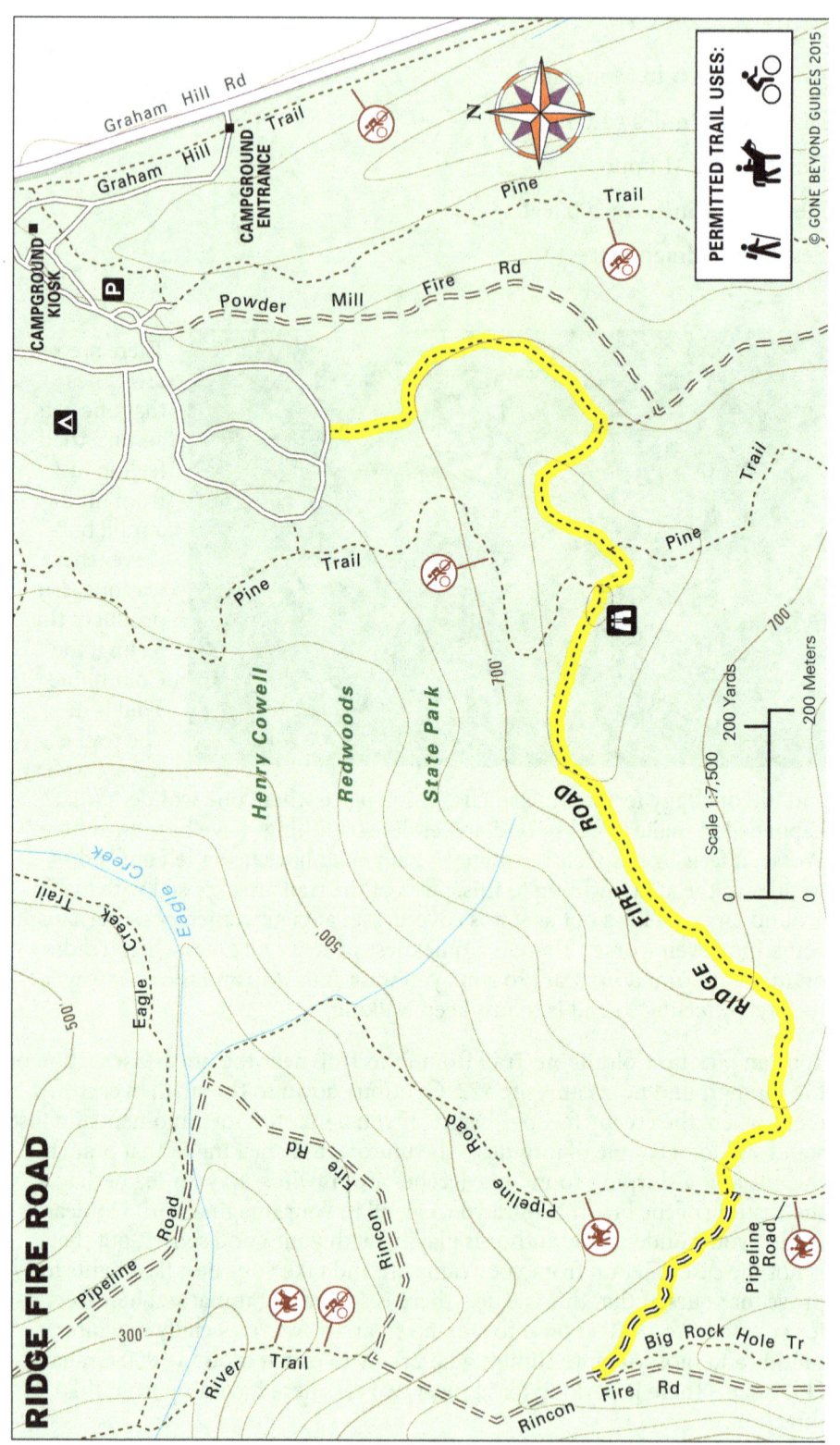

Ridge Fire Road

Difficulty: Moderate

Distance: 1.2 miles / 1.9 km

Duration: 1-2 hours

Elevation Gain/Loss: 125 feet

Best For: Great views of Monterey from the observation tower

The observation tower along Ridge Fire Road is certainly the highlight of this trail. It is a short distance from the campground and the main parking lot and as such is an attractive hike for many visitors. The view from the tower itself is worth the walk with stunning views as far south as Monterey. Perhaps even more stunning are the views north, east and west are also commanding, with the view inland showing some of the exposed Santa Cruz Sandhills, showing the extent of this ancient marine floor.

Much of Ridge Fire Road is on this ancient sand floor and in some areas the trail is becoming a narrow canal as folks cut through the soft almost sandy soil. Here the trees and vegetation look stunted and overall the area has an odd forlorn quality as the vegetation does what it can with the poor soils it has landed in.

Ridge Fire Road starts via Rincon Fire or Pipeline Roads and ends ultimately at the campground.

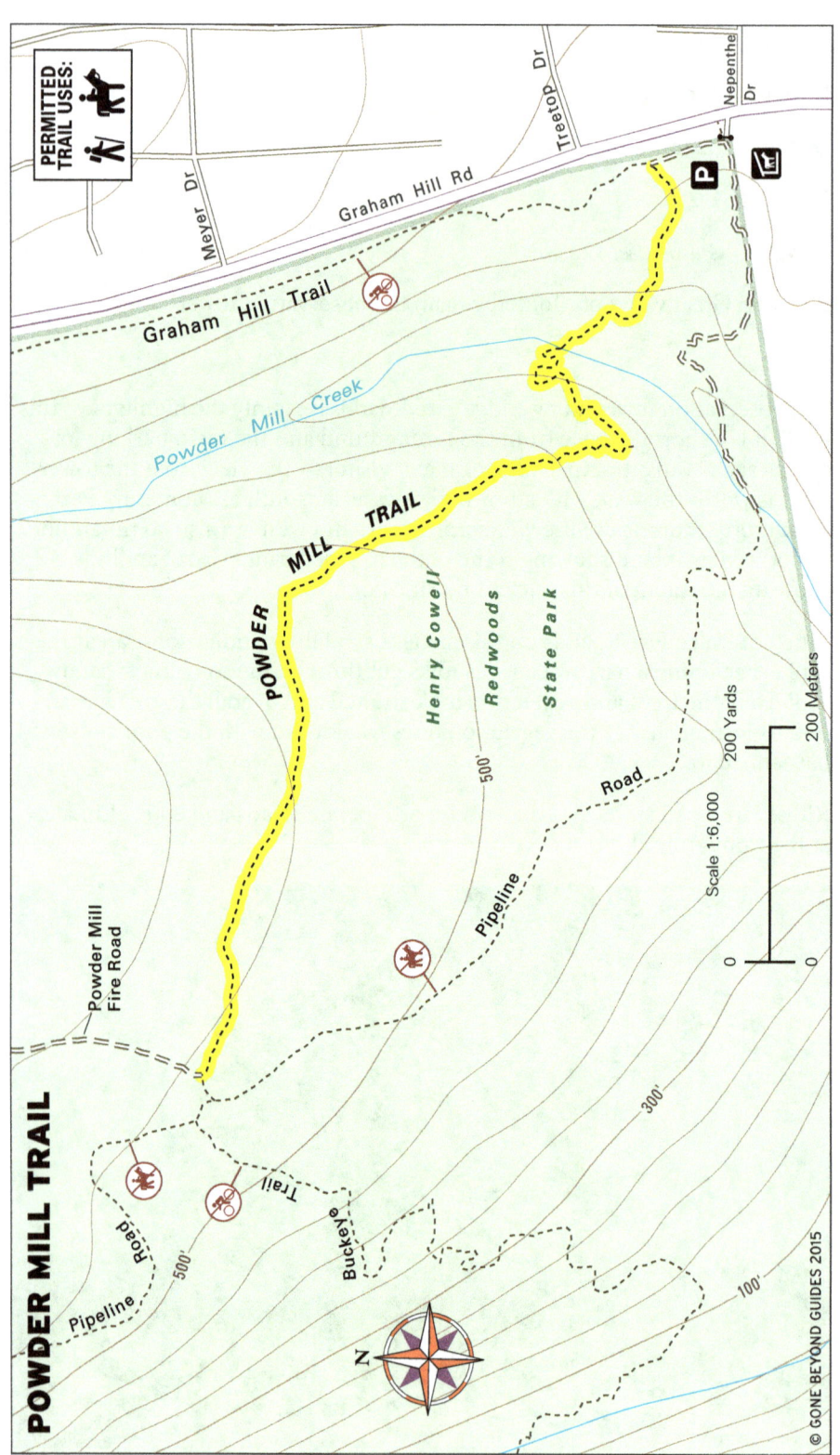

Powder Mill Trail

Difficulty: Moderate with steep sections

Distance: 0.7 miles / 1.1 km

Duration: 0.5 -1 hour

Elevation Gain/Loss: 250 feet

Best For: Making any southern hike into a loop.

The Powder Mill Trail, like its other namesake, Powder Mill Fire Road are named after the California Powder Works, which was a major employer in Santa Cruz manufacturing gunpowder in the late 1800's. The trail can be accessed just off Graham Hill Road at the southeastern corner of the park. Parking is available. Horse riding is allowed on all trails near this parking lot except Pipeline Road.

Once on the trail, it winds steeply down over a series of long switchbacks. Alternatively you can take a shortcut trail that will head even more steeply down where it meets up with Powder Mill Trail proper. The trail becomes less steep until ending at the 5 way junction with Powder Mill Fire Road, Pipeline Road and Buckeye Trail.

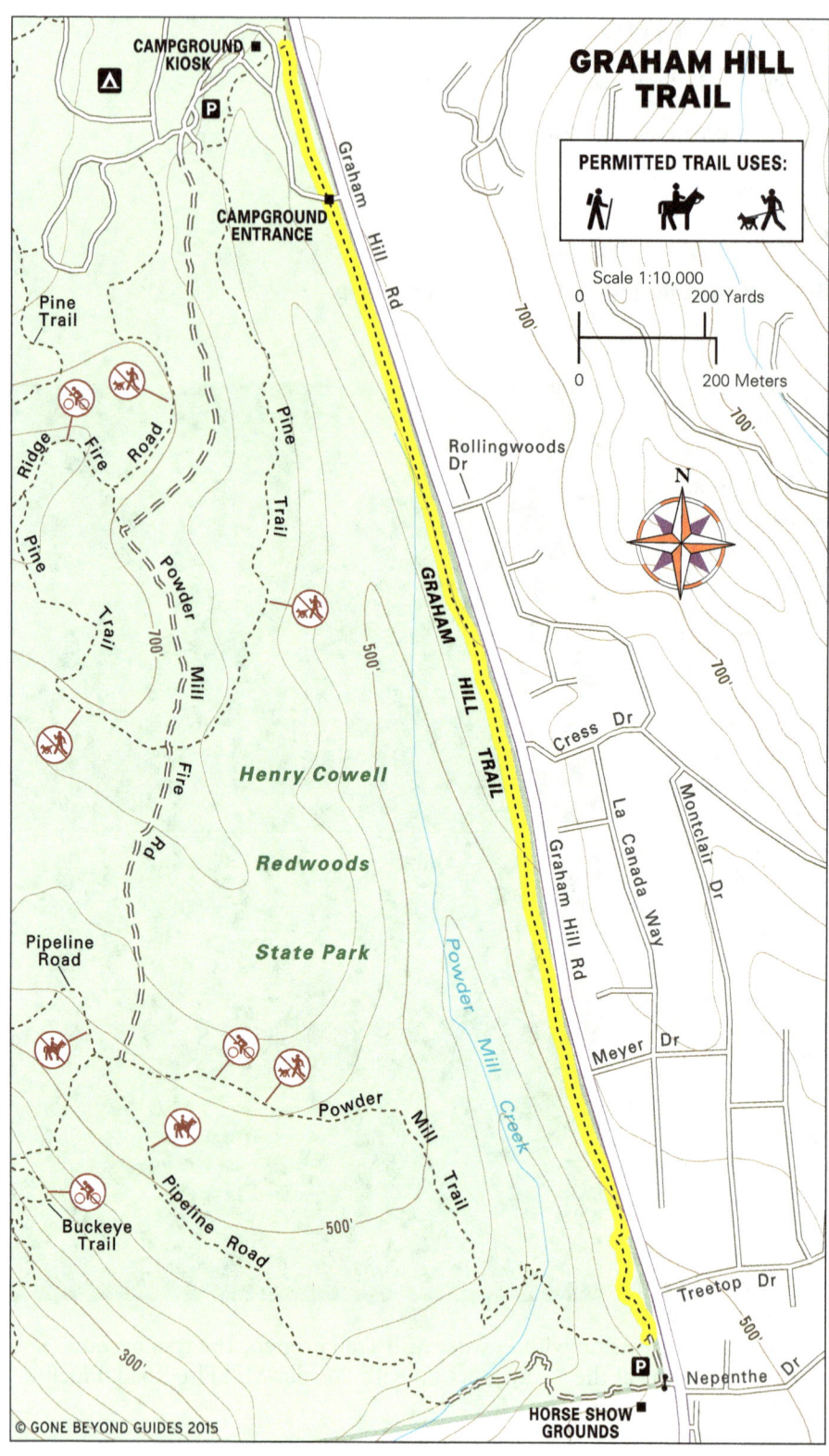

Graham Hill Trail

Difficulty: Easy, Moderate in sections

Distance: 1.4 miles / 2.3 km

Duration: 1-2 hours

Elevation Gain/Loss: 25 feet

Best For: Easy access jogging or taking Fido for a walk

Graham Hill Trail is a relatively flat wooded trail just off of Graham Hill Road. On the plus side, the trail's proximity to the road makes it an easy trail to pick up. It's also one of the few dog friendly trails in the park. This trail does connect with Pipeline Road which is equally dog friendly. Tying in Eagle Creek Trail does make the Graham Hill Trail/Pipeline Trail a loop, but unfortunately Fido is not allowed on Eagle Creek Trail.

The trail's proximity to the road is also one of its negatives. Graham Hill Road is a local thoroughfare as it makes for an easy route to Santa Cruz from Felton. As a result, the road is rather noisy, though the cars that pass by are heard more than they are seen. Parking can be had at either end of this section.

The trail is obviously marked, for the most part flat and can be muddy in the winter. It is marked for hiking, horses and dogs.

Trails in the Fall Creek Unit

Due to the easy access just off of the Felton Empire Road, there are several trail loops that are popular with visitors. To make the guide a bit easier to use, the Fall Creek Unit trails are split into two sections; those that are closer to the Felton Empire Road main parking lot and those that are not.

In general, all the Fall Creek Unit is designated mainly for hiking and horse usage. Dogs and mountain bikes are not allowed at all, and horses are restricted on a few trails. The Fall Creek Unit is an excellent spot for hikers, giving longer loops and varied scenery.

Trails of the Southern Portion

The trails within reach of the town of Felton are full of loops and offer visitors both creek side tranquility and decent hill climbs. For many that come to the Fall Creek Unit, this is as far as they go. That being said, this portion contains Fall Creek Trail, perhaps the nicest gem within the entire trail system of Henry Cowell. It also contains the richest deposits of history, with the remains of lime making quarries scattered along the Fall Creek Trail itself as well as other nearby trails.

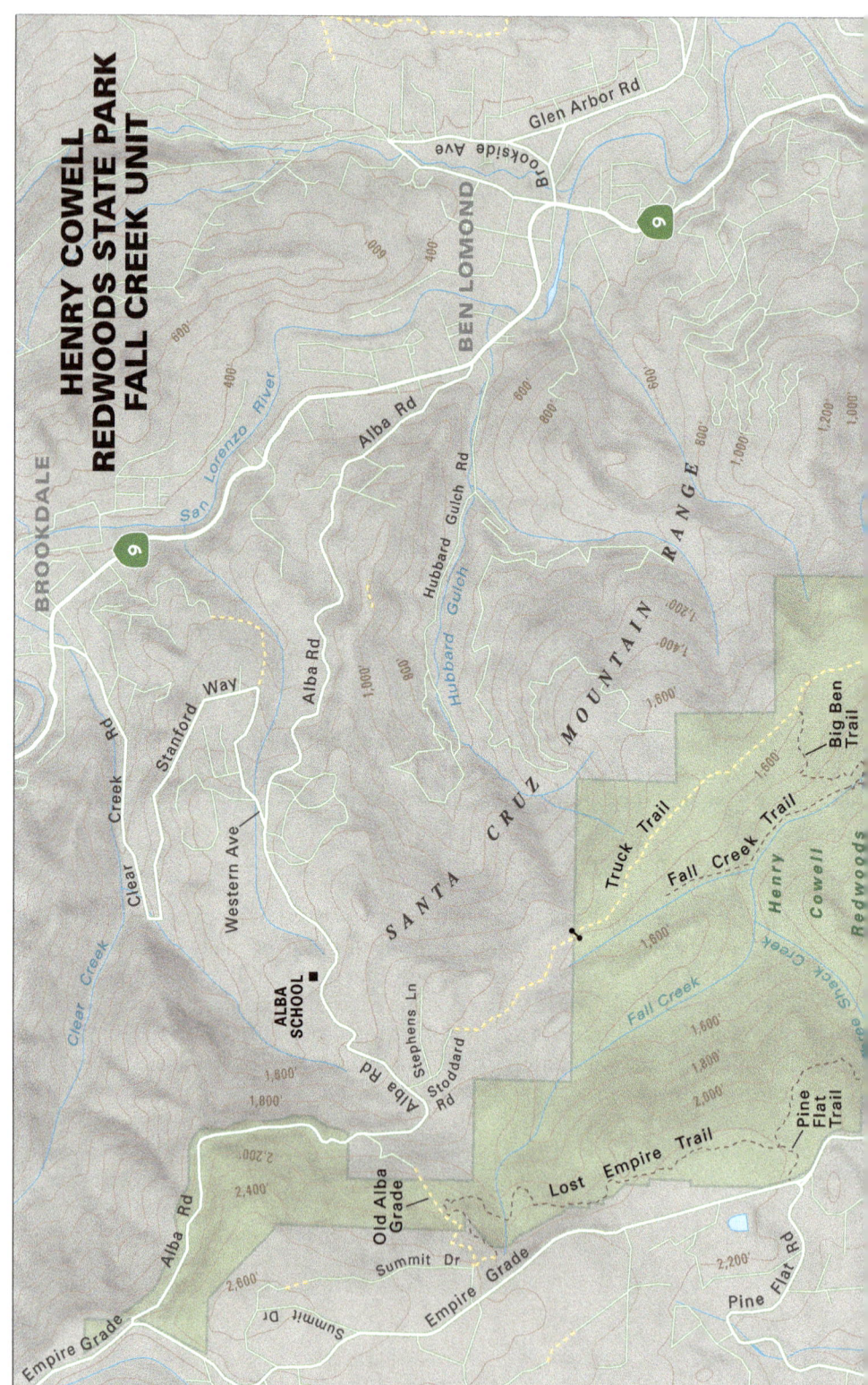

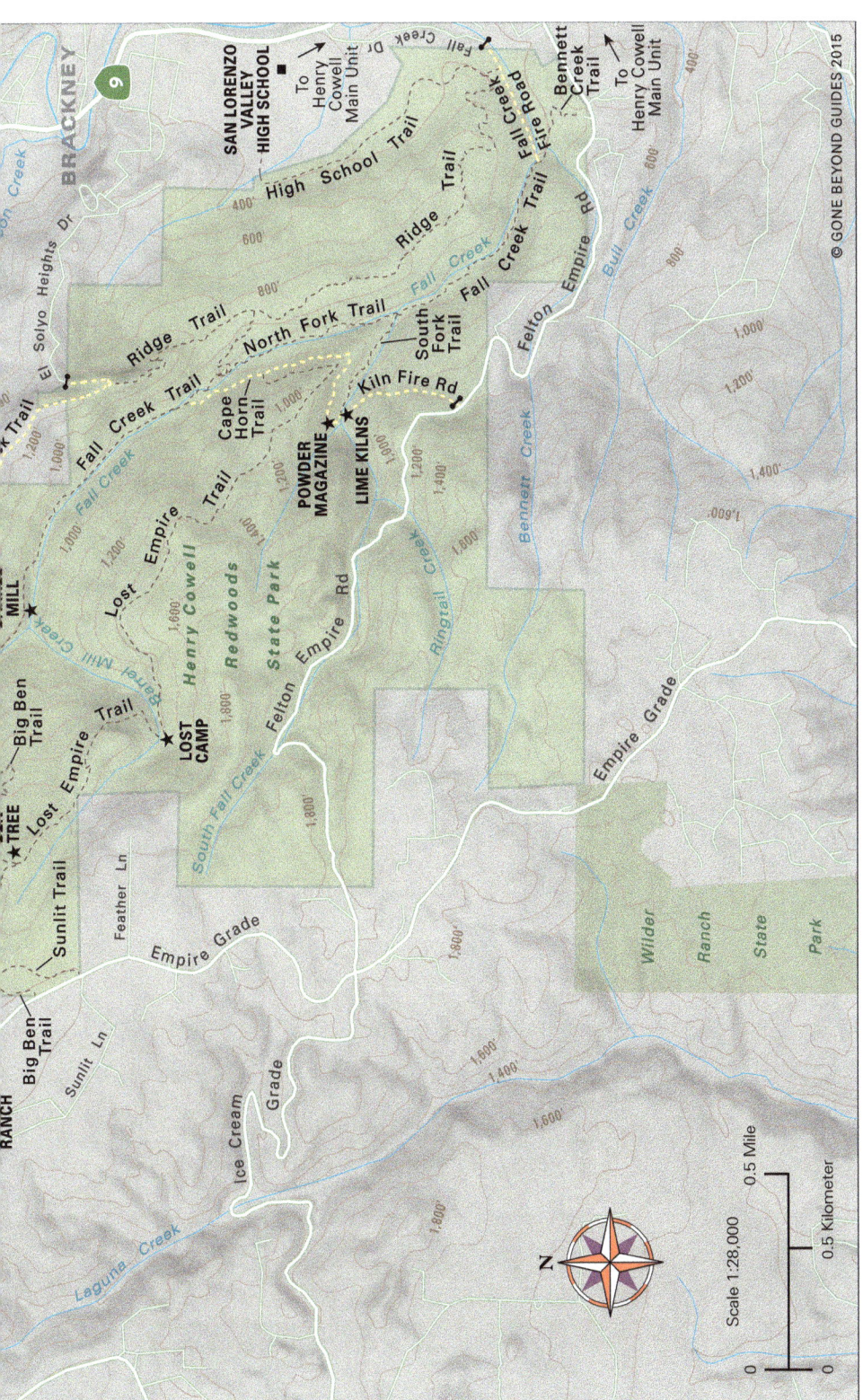

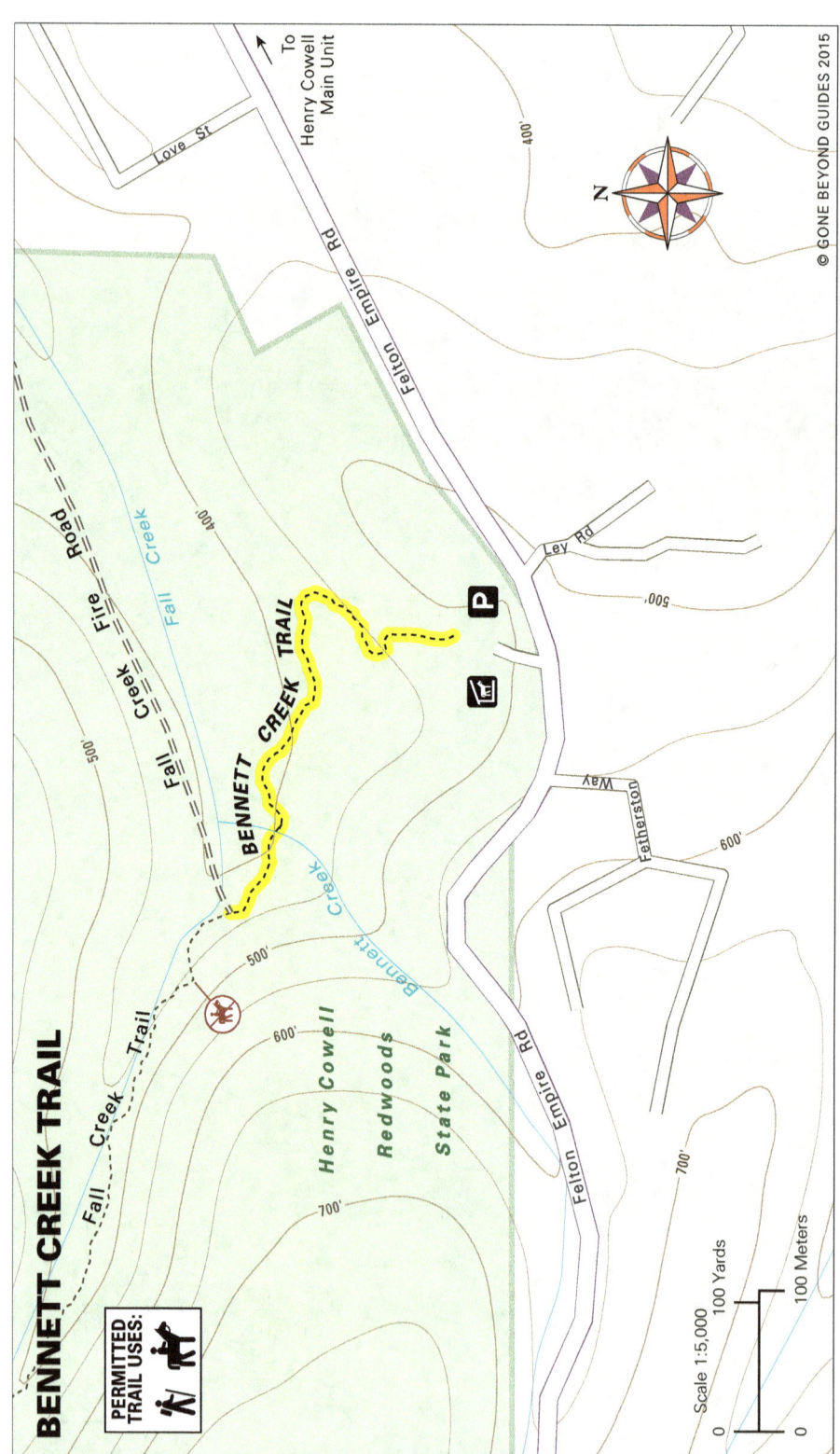

Bennett Creek Trail

Difficulty: Easy

Distance: 0.2 miles / 0.3 km

Duration: 10 minutes

Elevation Gain/Loss: 50 feet

Best For: Being the gateway to many of the major trails in Fall Creek.

Bennett Creek Trail starts at the Fall Creek Unit parking lot just 0.6 miles past Highway 9 on Felton Empire Road. The parking lot has room for about 20 cars and as the lot does get filled up by noon on weekends, cars are tucked into whatever parking spot is available. Come early if you want to ensure a spot as there is no other parking available in the nearby vicinity.

The trailhead is easy to spot winding down a short incline to Fall Creek. There is a nice view of the creek with a wide bridge as you near the water, a welcome introduction to what lies ahead for the visitor. There is a nice map kiosk just before the bridge to help you plan your hike. This trail is short and sweet, head to the left to jump onto the Fall Creek Trail or head across the bridge to begin Fall Creek Fire Road to High School and Ridge Trails.

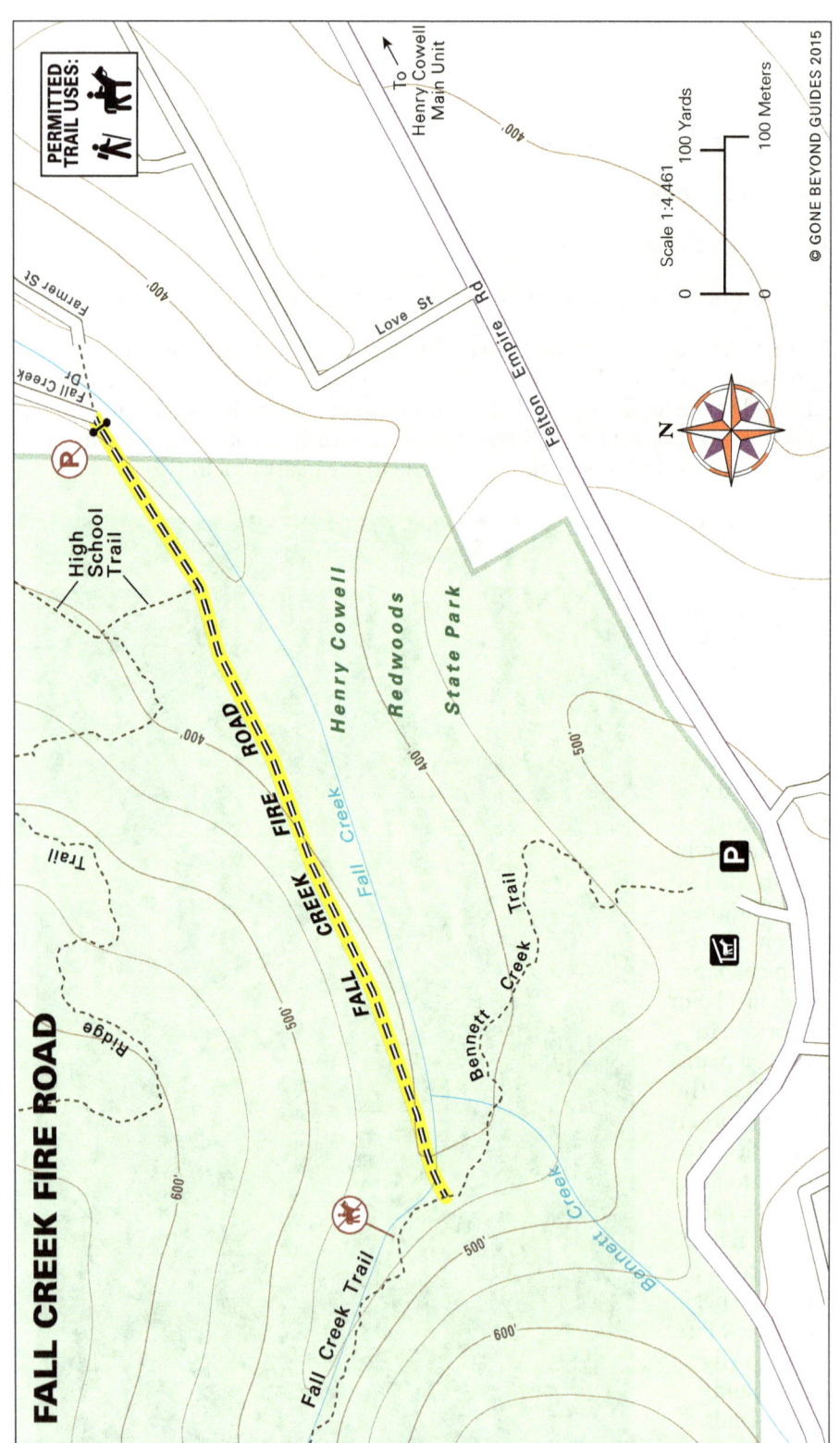

Fall Creek Fire Road

Difficulty: Easy

Distance: 0.3 miles / 0.5 km

Duration: 15-30 minutes

Elevation Gain: Level

Best For: Creek adventures off the path with the kids

Fall Creek Fire Road is not the trail you want if you wish to take up the very popular Fire Creek Trail. This wide old road starts at the bridge from Bennett Creek and goes for about 0.2 miles before intersecting with High School Trail. The road ends just after at the park's boundary.

Not much more to say about this old access road. It is a level easy grade. There are several informal trails that go to the creek. These areas vary from somewhat secluded banks to wide sandy bars next to a big foot bridge that are great for kids to explore. As always, poison oak is around, so be watchful.

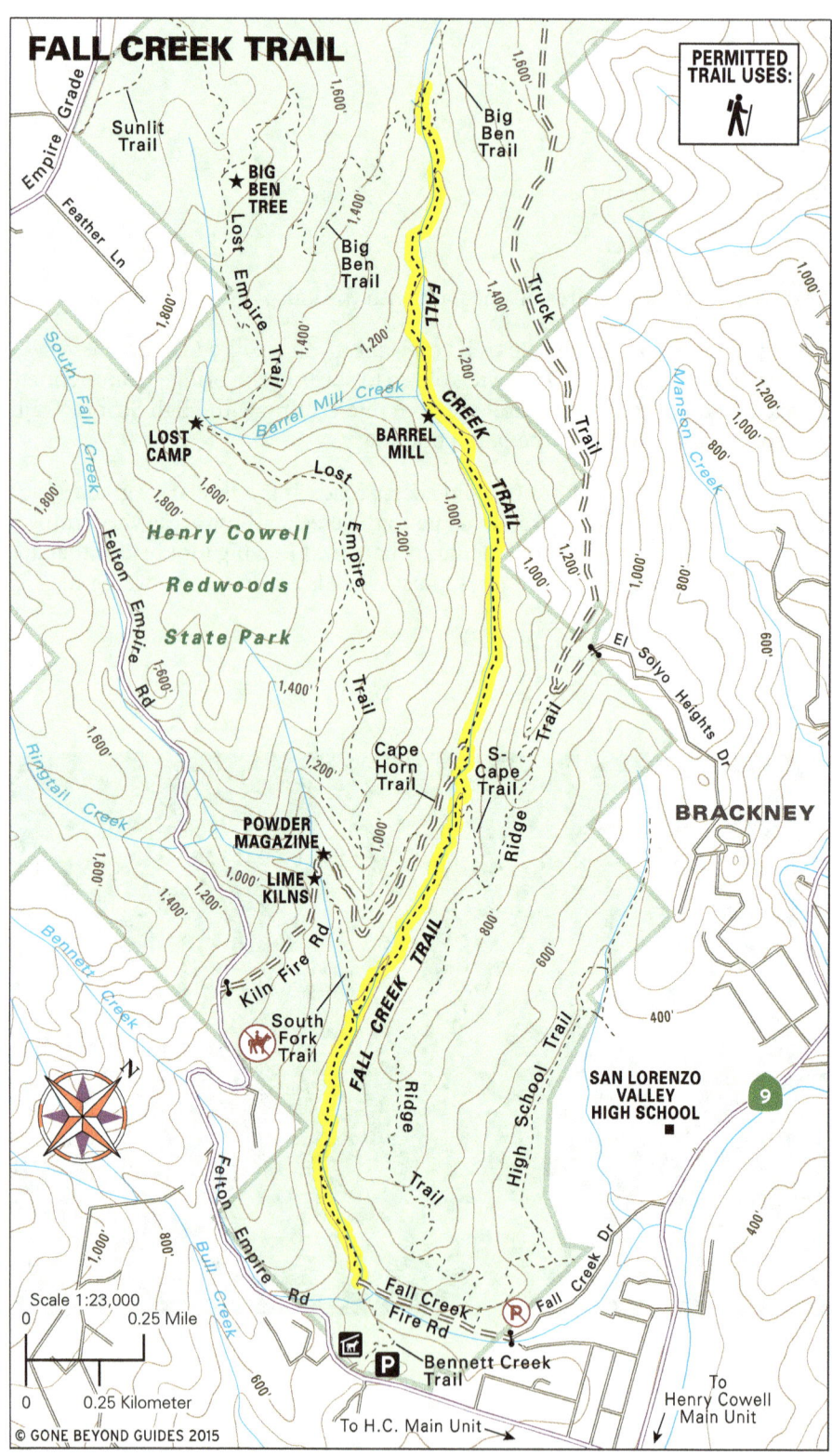

Fall Creek Trail

Difficulty: Easy to gently moderate

Distance: 3.6 miles / 5.8 km

Duration: 2-4 hours

Elevation Gain/Loss: 1000 feet

Best For: Families and hikers looking for a fairly easy hike in the redwoods near a clear creek.

Fall Creek Trail has a warm heart. The trail itself is sure footed, climbing gradually through a cathedral of second growth redwoods, a few old growth redwoods, Douglas-fir and other evergreens. There are foot bridges to help you get across the handful of creek crossings. Then there is the creek itself. It gives views of small waterfalls, gentle rapids, wide sandy spits that elbow around the turns of the canyon. The water is crystal clear and inviting as it flows. Occasionally there is a fallen tree, now mossy and in decay that crosses the creek, daring the adventurous to navigate across it.

In one spot, a tree has fallen right in between two others, with its root system right by the trail side to give the hiker a view of what shallow little bunch of roots actually hold up these massive trees. In another spot, just beyond a foot bridge between South Fork and South Cape Trails, there are visible lines in the canyon walls showing past high water marks, one 7 feet high. If you do find the line, trace it across to the other side of this narrow canyon section to see just how much water can flow through this small watershed.

The trail gradually climbs up the creek's canyon, at times in a moderately steep fashion, for the most part, the climb is gentle enough. From Bennett Trail your first junction will be at the South Fork Trail. Stay to your right across the small footbridge on the North Fork of the Fall Creek Trail (note the signs actually call this North Fork Trail). For families with smaller children, this bridge makes for a good stopping point. The trail continues to afford views of the creek till you hit the South Cape Trail. Horses are allowed to continue on the South Cape Trail but are not allowed further up the Fall Creek Trail. This area is a junction for Cape Horn Trail as well. As of this writing, while the junction itself can be confusing, the trail is very well marked. A short 0.8 mile distance further up the trail brings the hiker to the Barrel Mill Area. There is a small descriptive sign explaining the site and is well worth a visit. There is a remarkably well preserved stave machine as well as other remnants of machinery used to making the lime transport barrels.

Lime production required full time barrel makers to craft the packaging of the lime. This outdoor workshop operated from 1912 to 1925 and had a functioning saw and other machinery all powered by the creek itself. There are enough remnants left over to almost piece together how they used water to power the stave and barrel head maker.

Like most of the water powered devices of this era, you simply needed a Pelton wheel and enough water pressure to drive it to operate machinery. Essentially, a flume was created up stream to divert Fall Creek's water downstream to the Pelton wheel. The Pelton wheel is a water wheel but its design is far superior to other types of devices during this period. As the water travelled down the flume, it would pick up speed and thus energy. On hitting the Pelton wheel, nearly all of the water's energy was transferred to the wheel. This transferred energy allowed the Pelton wheel to spin. A worker would then use a drive shaft and leather pulleys to turn other items of machinery, such as the stave and the barrel head saw.

As intensive and ingenious as this seems, it was but a part of a bigger operation. Above the Barrel Mill Area a saw mill cut the raw redwoods into manageable blocks. From these raw blocks, the Barrel Mill machinery then made the parts of the barrel and sent them further downstream by oxen where a cooperage assembled the parts into the final barrel. From here they were loaded with lime and transported for shipment primarily to San Francisco to use in making mortar and plaster.

Once past the Barrel Mill Area, the trail continues to ascend for another 0.6 miles before petering out to a more informal trail. It is possible to continue to navigate up the Fall Creek watershed to Pine Flat Trail, however the trail is informal at best and not present for much of this true bush whacking experience.

Towards the official end of Fall Creek Trail, it does intersect the unmarked Big Ben Trail. Big Ben does not cross Fall Creek Trail in a straight line. The lower right fork is about 0.1 mile from the upper left fork. Neither are marked.

In regards to the two loops that can be had with Fall Creek, both are a little more than 9 miles and either Fall Creek to Lost Empire or Fall Creek to Truck Trail are very rewarding hikes. Going up Fall Creek Trail seems to allow more time to take in the creek side scenery.

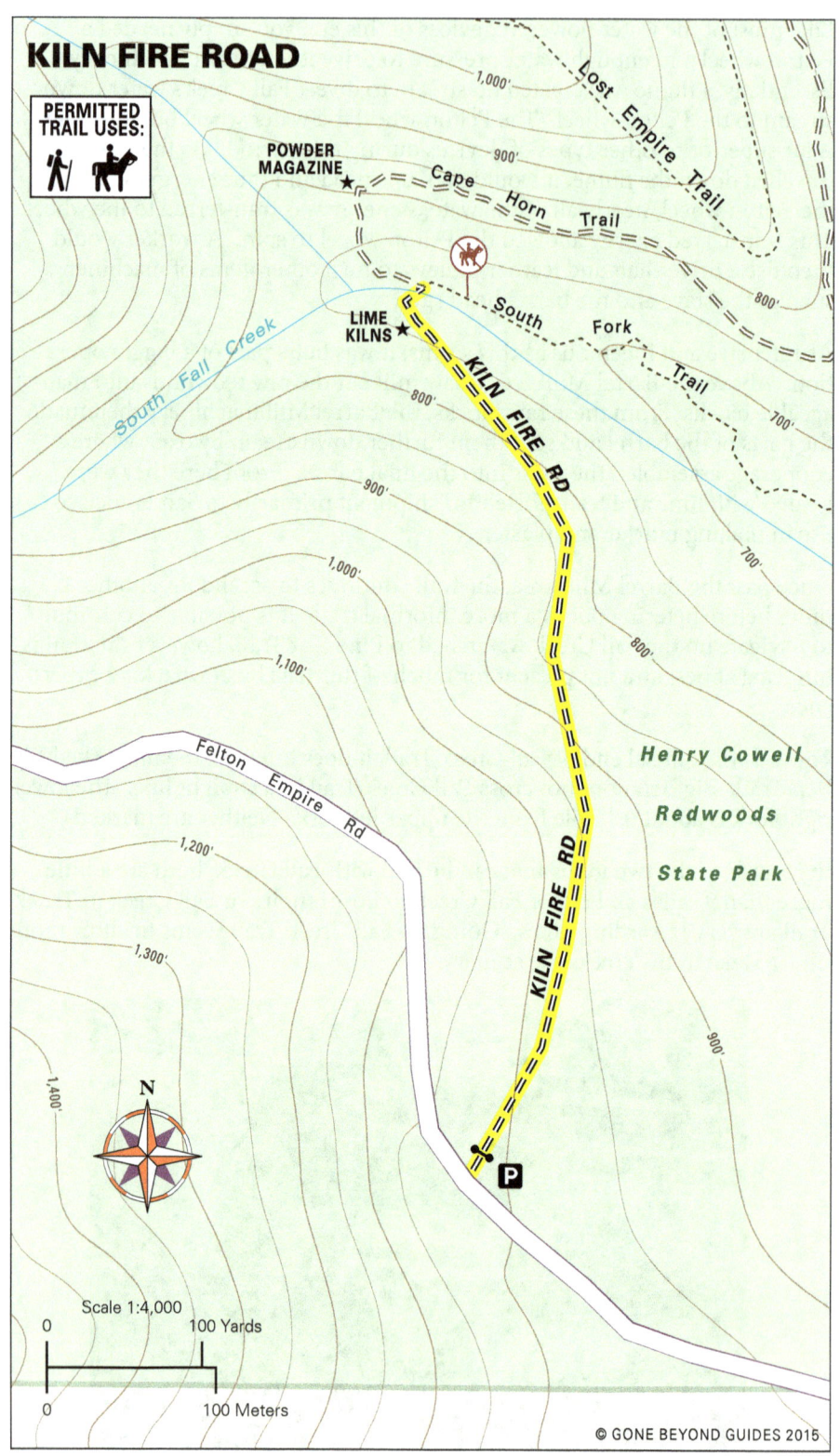

Kiln Fire Road

Difficulty: Moderately steep

Distance: 0.5 miles / 0.8 km

Duration: 15 -45 minutes

Elevation Gain/Loss: 500 feet

Best For: Quick access to the Lime Kiln Ruins

The Kiln Fire Road is located about 1.7 miles up Felton Empire Road from the intersection with Highway 9. There is parking for 2-3 cars and is not well marked. Look for a sign coming up Feltong Empire Grade denoting the park's boundary, the parking will be shortly after this sign on your right hand side.

Kiln Fire Road itself is easily found just past the gate from the parking area. It goes steeply down or conversely, makes for a nice uphill climb coming back from a long hike. A loop starting at Kiln Fire Road, going up Lost Empire Trail, across Big Ben Trail and back down Fall Creek Trail is just over 9 miles.

Besides using it as launching points for longer loops, it is the quickest way to get to the lime kiln ruins. While short, it is moderately steep and may be a challenge for young children.

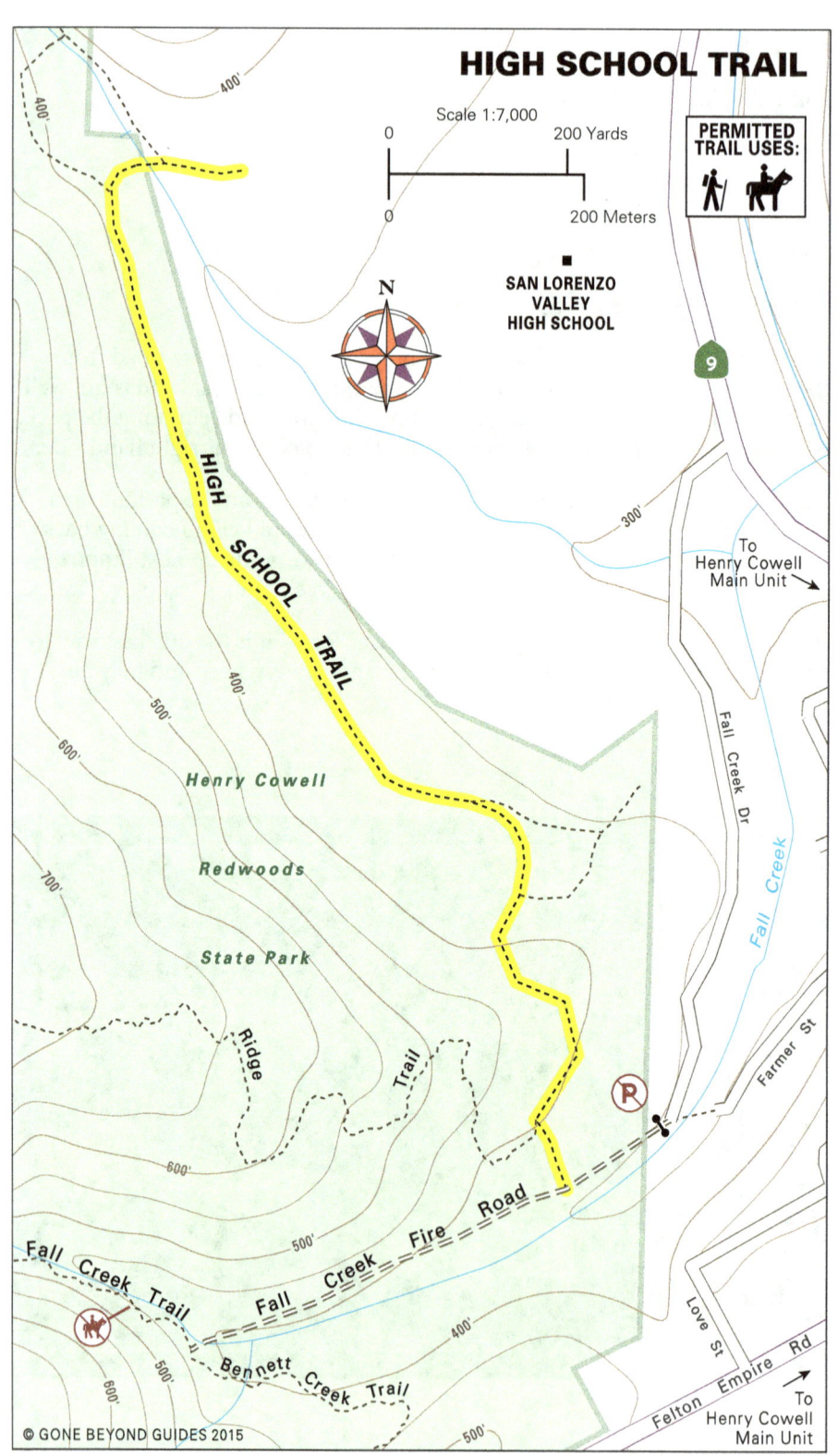

High School Trail

Difficulty: Easy

Distance: 1.1 miles / 1.8 km

Duration: 1-2 hours

Elevation Gain/Loss: 50 feet

Best For: Hanging out after school.

High School Trail is named after the San Lorenzo High School that sits below it. From the Fall Creek Fire Road it stays fairly flat travelling nicely through second growth redwood and some mixed evergreen. The trail is one of the only flat hikes in the park and is more redwood than mixed evergreen. This enjoyable little hike ultimately ends at the high school.

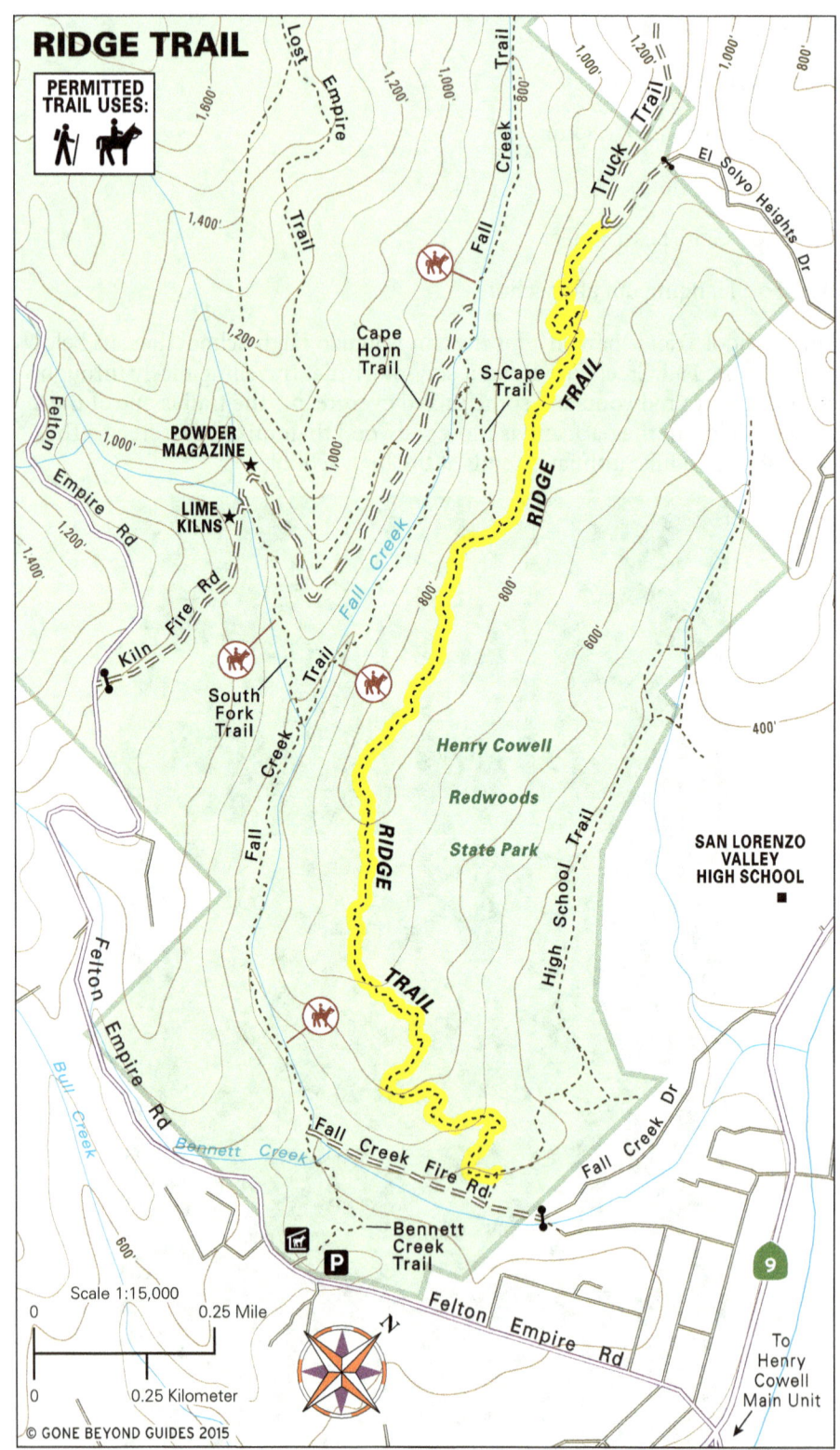

Ridge Trail

Difficulty: Steep

Distance: 1.6 miles / 2.6 km

Duration: 1-3 hours

Elevation Gain/Loss: 700 feet

Best For: Enjoying a deep forest feeling while hiking

The Ridge Trail can be picked up either by the connecting Truck Trail or by driving to the alternate parking area at the end of El Soyo Heights Drive. This single track hike is steep in sections, travelling through second growth mixed evergreens. Towards the upper end of the Ridge Trail, there are several nice views of the surrounding Santa Cruz Mountains that peek through the trees. At one point the trail goes through sandy terrain similar to the Santa Cruz sandhills found in the Main Unit of Henry Cowell. While the trees in some sections appear to be stunted, the soil does appear to have done a better job of establishing itself then the true sand hills of the main unit. The trail becomes more wooded and with diminishing views as you head downward.

If you are looking for a loop from Fall Creek Trail, cutting up Big Ben Trail to Truck Trail to Ridge Trail is a nice way to go. Fall Creek Trail is gradual to moderate up, Big Ben is a steep but relatively short pitch and the hike back to the car is almost entirely downhill once you meet up with Truck Trail.

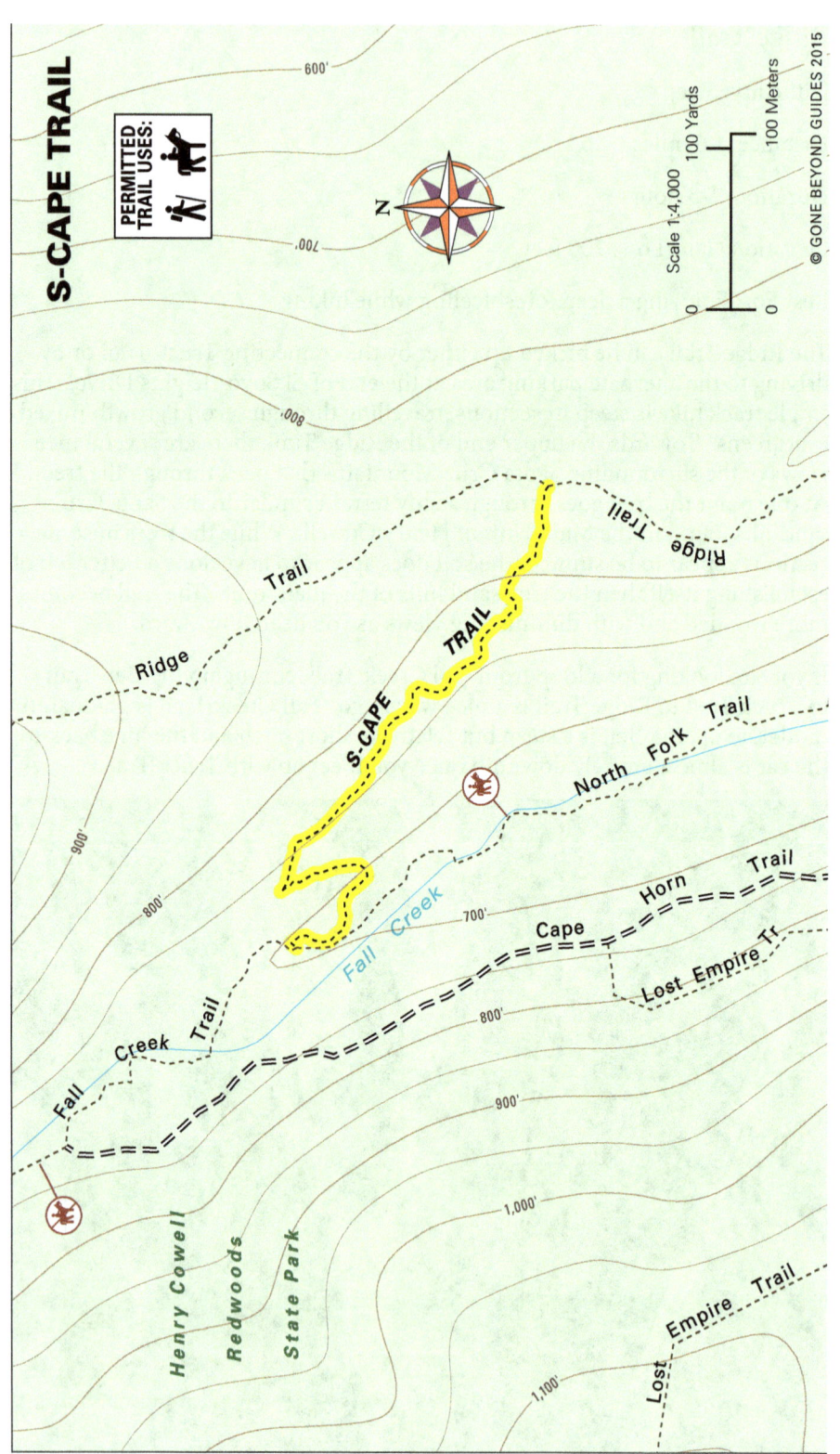

S-Cape Trail

Difficulty: Steep at times

Distance: 0.3 miles / 0.5 km

Duration: 15 -30 minutes

Elevation Gain/Loss: 125 feet

Best For: A shorter loop from Fall Creek Trail up the canyon and back to your car.

The S-Cape Trail is an extension of the Cape Horn Trail connecting the visitor from the Fall Creek Trail to the Ridge Trail. The trail climbs rather steeply at times from the lower creek floor up to the ridge. At the creek the S-Cape Trail merges for a bit with the Fall Creek Trail.

S-Cape is a great way to see a decent portion of Fall Creek if you are pressed for time and can't do one of the longer loops. Start on Fall Creek Trail, staying on the North Fork of Fall Creek and then looping on S-Cape to Ridge for the return via Fall Creek Fire Road.

Note that if coming from the Truck Trail, you will see a trail marked with branches. This is not the S-Cape Trail but an unofficial trail that does lead to Fall Creek, near the Barrel Mill Area.

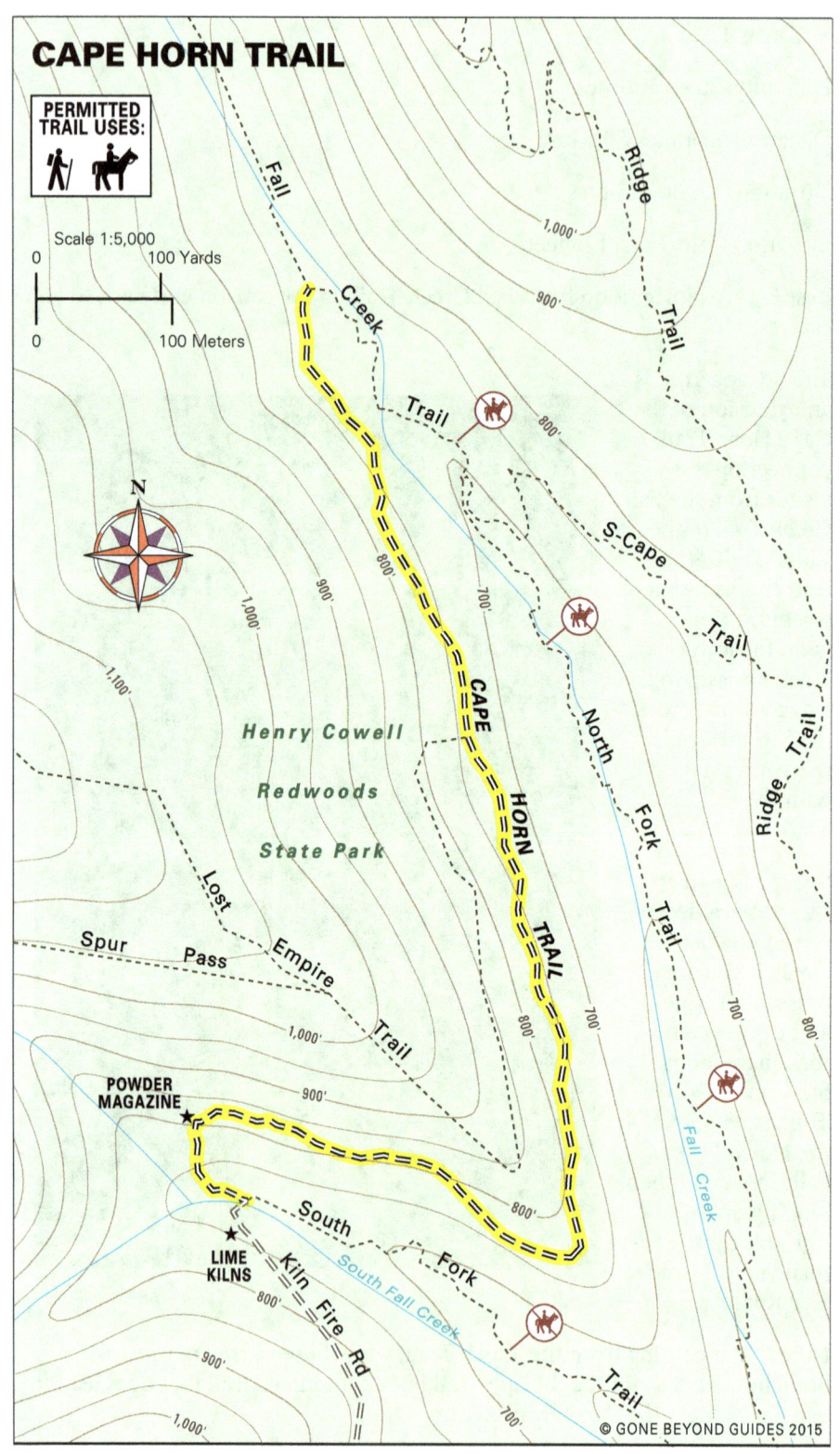

Cape Horn Trail

Difficulty: Steep in sections

Distance: 0.7 miles / 1.1 km

Duration: 0.5 to 1 hour

Elevation Gain/Loss: 100 feet

Best For: Finding the Powder Magazine

Cape Horn is an old wagon road that connects the Lime Kiln area with Fall Creek. If taking Cape Horn to connect to the Lost Empire Trail, you will notice on the map that the two trails parallel each other for a bit. There is an obvious but unofficial trail connector to shave off this piece of trail, however taking this connector will undoubtedly cause you to miss out on the namesake for the trail, whose sharp bend was reminiscent of the pioneers own journeys from the east, sailing around Cape Horn to California.

The IXL Lime Kiln ruins lie at the south western end Cape Horn Trail. The ruins are in fairly good shape and three lime kilns can be easily made out. The ruins are fenced off so do be mindful that they are in a state of arrested decay. The entire area is a pleasant little green nook with patches of sorrel along the banks of the south fork of Fall Creek that passes through the site.

Just past the kilns is a Powder Magazine where the lime rock blasting dynamite was stored. The storage area is little more than a small cave cut into the base of the hill. If you are curious yet not adventurous enough to get on your hands and knees to look inside the Powder Magazine, it doesn't go back very far. If however you are equally curious and adventurous, the cave extends deep into the hillside and holds vast untold riches that only you will find.

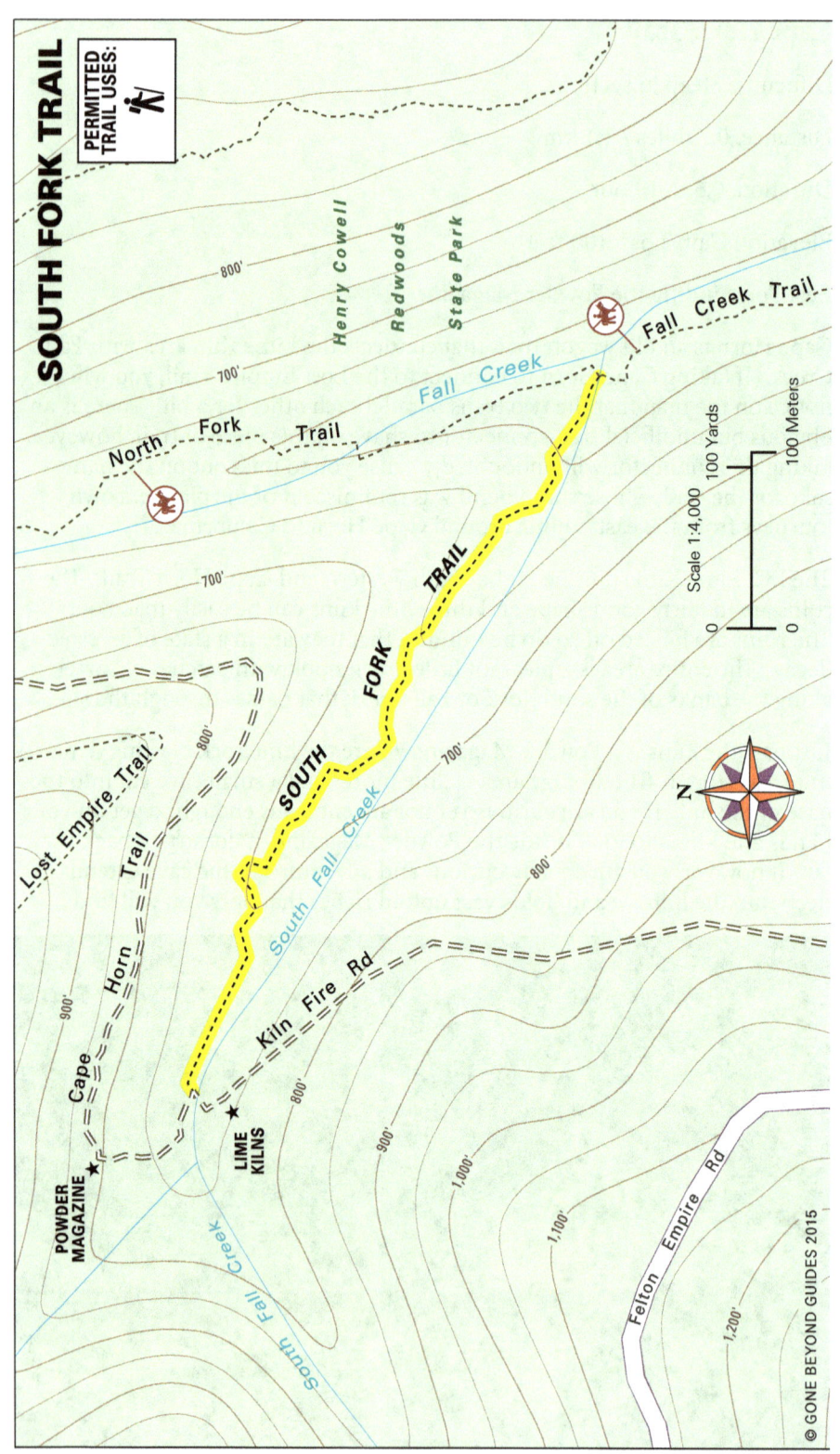

South Fork Trail

Difficulty: Easy

Distance: 0.4 miles / 0.6 km

Duration: 15 -30 minutes

Elevation Gain/Loss: 50 feet

Best For: An alternate but equally peaceful creek side hike.

This short trail is found at the juncture of the North and South Forks of Fall Creek if coming from the Empire Grade Road parking lot. The Fall Creek to South Fork Trail will take the visitor straight to the Lime Kiln area and is perfect for a moderate family hike. Families with smaller children may find that getting to the creek juncture itself is long enough.

The South Fork Trail is slightly steeper than the North Fork over the same area. If you do take the South Fork Trail to visit the lime kilns and want to connect back to the main Fall Creek Trail, taking the Cape Horn Trail will deposit you back on the Fall Creek Trail. Allow time for the lime kiln ruins, they are worth exploring.

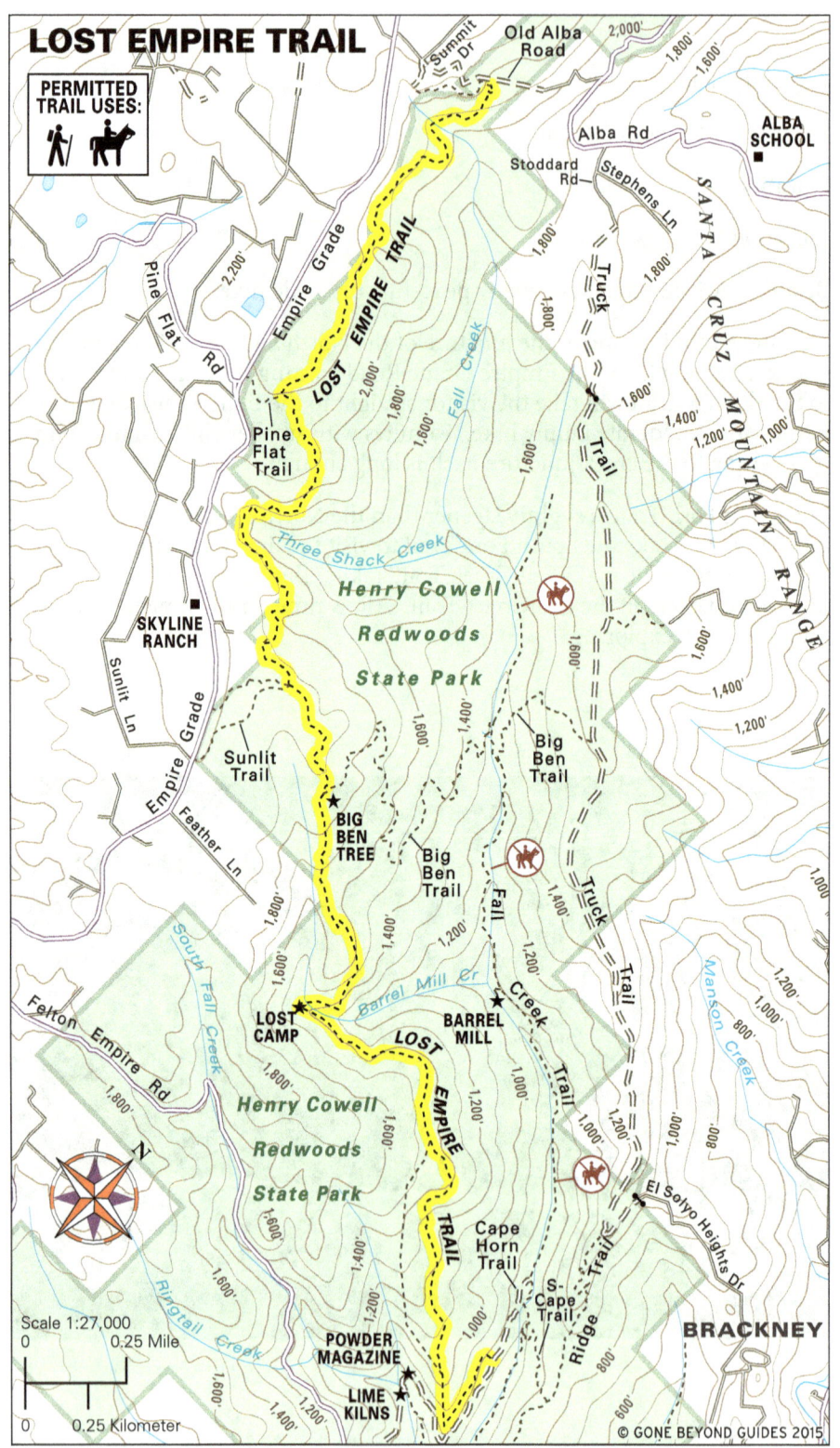

Trails of the Mid and Northern Portion

The trails within the middle and northern sections of the Fall Creek Unit offer the visitor longer hikes to tackle. These sections are typically less used and thus more secluded. It is possible to connect to the Lost Empire Trail via public transportation, allowing a long hiking opportunity back to Felton.

Lost Empire Road

Difficulty: Steep and strenuous

Distance: 4.8 miles / 7.7 km

Duration: 2-4 hours

Elevation Gain/Loss: 1300 feet

Best For: Horses, oxen and strong hikers

The Henry Cowell docent guide advises that this steep trail is recommended more for horses than hikers. It is strenuous, but certainly within the realms of doable for strong ramblers. The single track trail goes through mixed evergreen forests for the most part with an occasional small grove of redwoods. It also passes the Big Ben old growth redwood tree. The trail was used by oxen to carry firewood for the lime kilns. This is a fairly remote area of the park and mountain lion tracks have been spotted along the trail.

For those looking to connect to Big Ben Trail, don't be confused with the unmarked trail near Lost Camp. This trail is an unofficial downhill jaunt connecting the visitor to the Barrel Mill Area via Barrel Mill Creek. The Big Ben Trail is still a ways farther up the hill.

Lost Empire Trail continues uphill to Old Alba Trail, the northernmost reaches of the park. You can hook into Lost Empire from Sunlit and Pine Flat Trails.

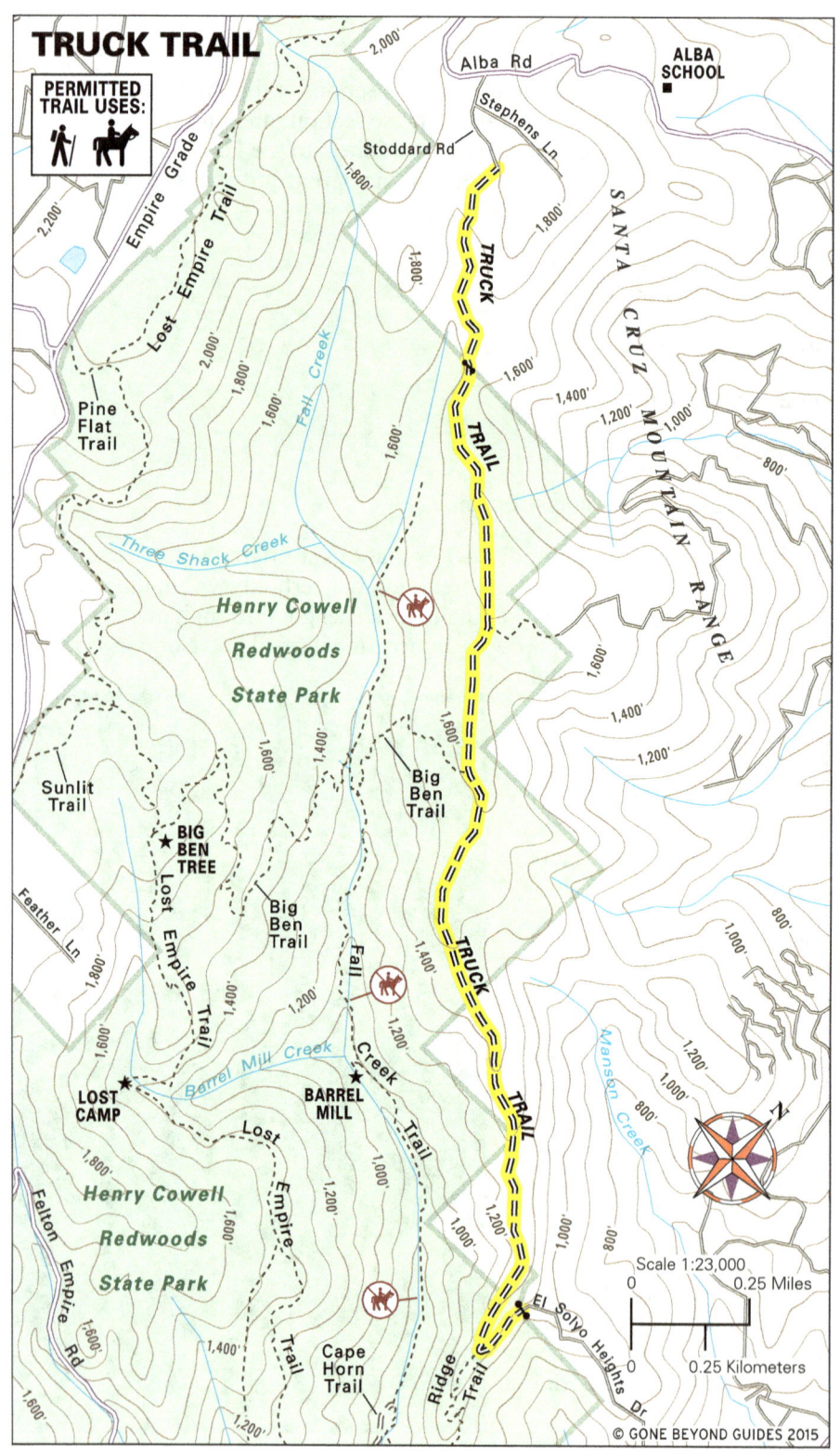

Truck Trail

Difficulty: Steep and Strenuous

Distance: 2.5 miles / 4.0 km

Duration: 1-3 hours

Elevation Gain/Loss: 800 feet

Best For: Hiking without having to look down too much.

Truck Trail can be picked up either via Big Ben Trail or by driving to the alternate parking area at the end of El Soyo Heights Drive. The best part of Truck Trail is that it is a wide old access road making it easy to navigate. It can be steep in sections going consistently up or downhill depending on the direction of travel. The Truck Trail does travel outside of the park's boundaries onto private property but other than one locked gate along this section, it's hard to notice any difference. Good views of the Santa Cruz Mountains can be seen through the trees.

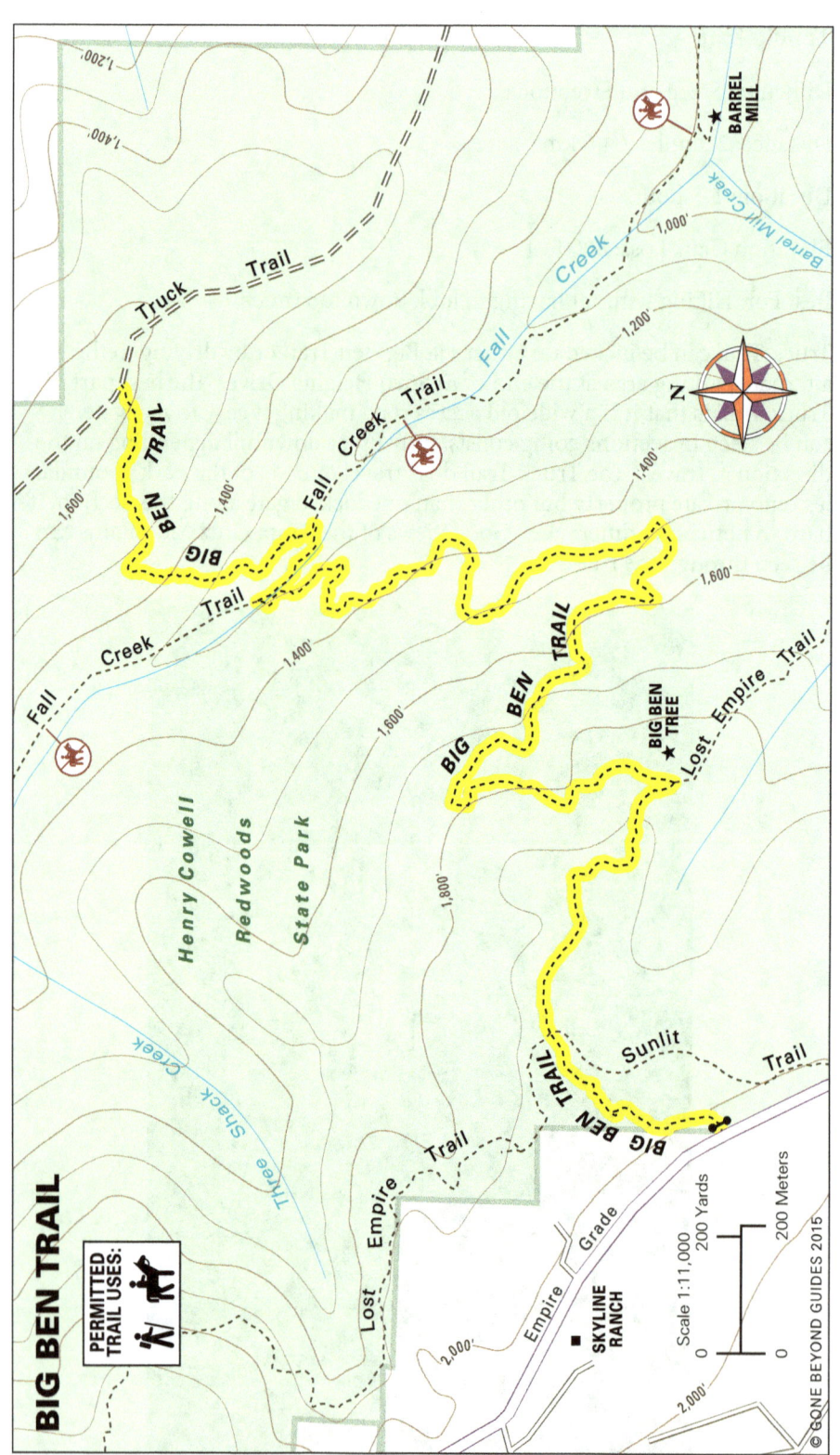

Big Ben Trail

Difficulty: Steep and strenuous

Distance: 1.9 miles / 3.1 km

Duration: 1-3 hours

Elevation Gain/Loss: 700 feet

Best For: Creating a loop out of the Fall Creek Trail.

Big Ben Trail is hilly, steep at times and strenuous. If you are trying to create a loop hike from the end of Fall Creek Trail, take the right fork up Big Ben to Truck Trail. The other option is to take Big Ben left to the Lost Empire Trail.

The right and left junctions of Big Ben from Fall Creek are about 0.1 miles from each other with the right junction being the lower of the two. Neither junction is marked, though both are fairly easy to spot.

The junction leading to the Truck Trail is steep but relatively short. It ends at the obvious Truck Trail though the junction is not marked. Locals have set up rock cairns and some day glow tape to mark the trail.

Going in the other direction, the trail climbs again steeply out of the Fall Creek watershed via a series of switchbacks to Lost Empire Trail. The Big Ben Tree sits at this junction and is named after the nearby town of Ben Lomond. Be sure to venture to the back side of the Big Ben Tree for a pleasant surprise. This trail is a rather new one and was built by the Santa Cruz Mountains Horesman's Association.

If you do plan to make a loop hike out of Fall Creek using Big Ben, the full distance of the loop either way is a little over 9 miles and is definitely more strenuous if you decided to travel down Fall Creek.

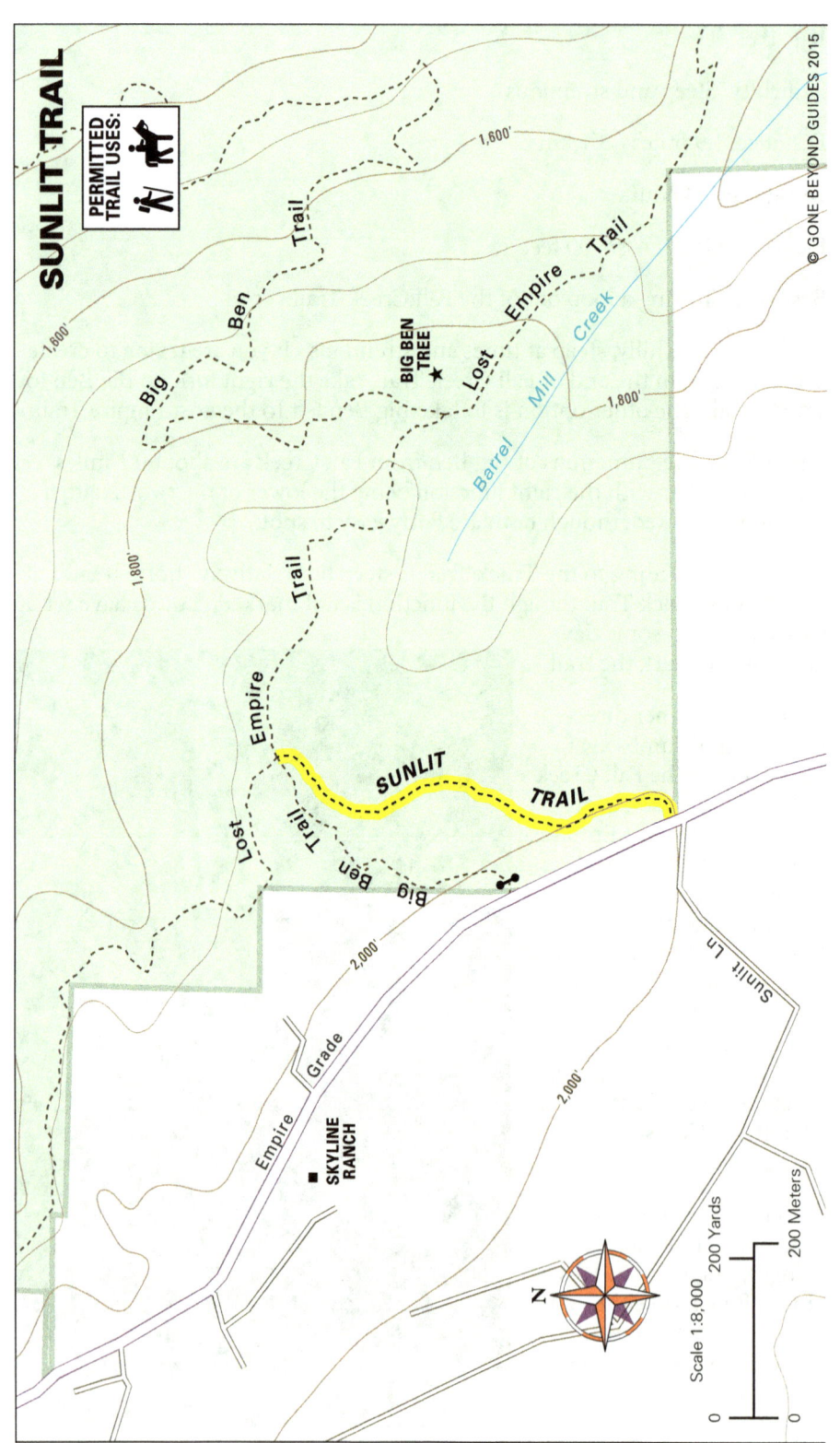

Sunlit Trail

Difficulty: Easy

Distance: 0.3 miles / 0.5 km

Duration: 15-30 minutes

Elevation Gain/Loss: 100 feet

Best For: Taking the road not taken.

Sunlit Trail provides easy access to the Lost Empire and Big Ben Trails. There are two trails in this area, one called Sunlit Trail and another unnamed trail further north which shall be dubbed as Sunlit North Trail for purposes of this description.

Sunlit Trail is fairly easy to find, though the trail head itself is marked only with a small sign indicating what is not allowed on the park (dogs and bikes). Sunlit Trail is 4.5 miles from Felton Empire Road at Highway 9. Head up Felton Empire Road and make a right on Empire Grade. Sunlit trail is just past Sunlit Road on your right hand side. The trail is just above the bus stop, which makes for an easy jump off via public transit for local visitors. There is a small amount of room on the shoulder for parking but it is tight.

The Big Ben Trail is another tenth of a mile up the road from Sunlit Trail. The trail is marked by a locked gate which leads to an old fire road. There is ample parking at this trailhead though opposite of the trail are residential homes, so be mindful of blocking driveways.

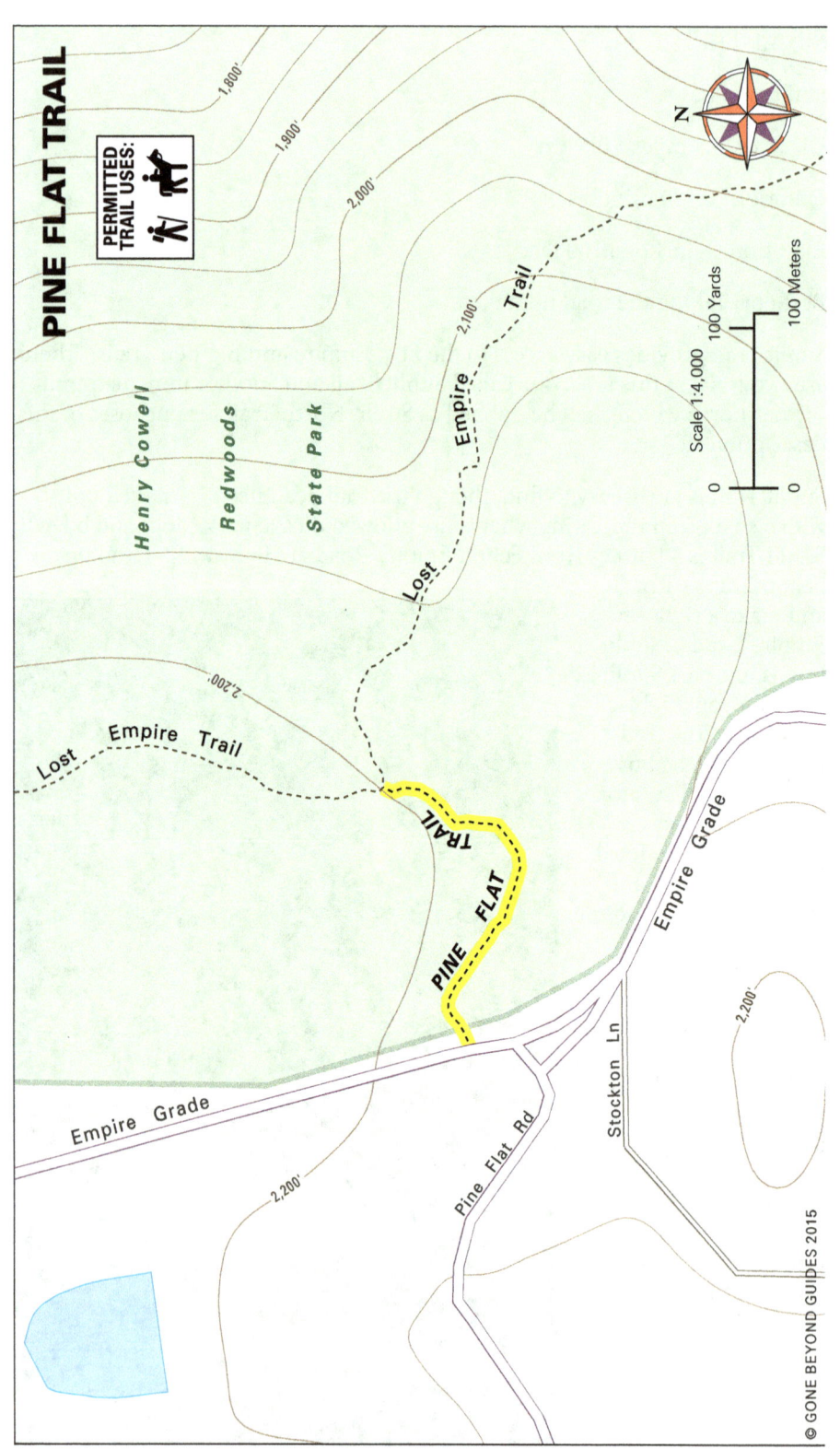

Pine Flat Trail

Difficulty: Easy

Distance: 0.2 miles / 0.3 km

Duration: 15-30 minutes

Elevation Gain/Loss: 50 feet

Best For: Finding a quick access to the Lost Empire Trail.

Pine Flat Trail gives the hiker a quick way to get into the upper reaches of Lost Empire Trail. The Trailhead is 5.4 miles from Felton Empire Road at Highway 9. Head up Felton Empire Road and continue right on Empire Grade until you get to Pine Flat Road.

The trailhead is not obviously marked but is fairly straightforward to locate. It will be just after passing Pine Flat Road on your right, directly across from a "Slippery When Wet" sign. In the same area as the sign there is parking for several cars.

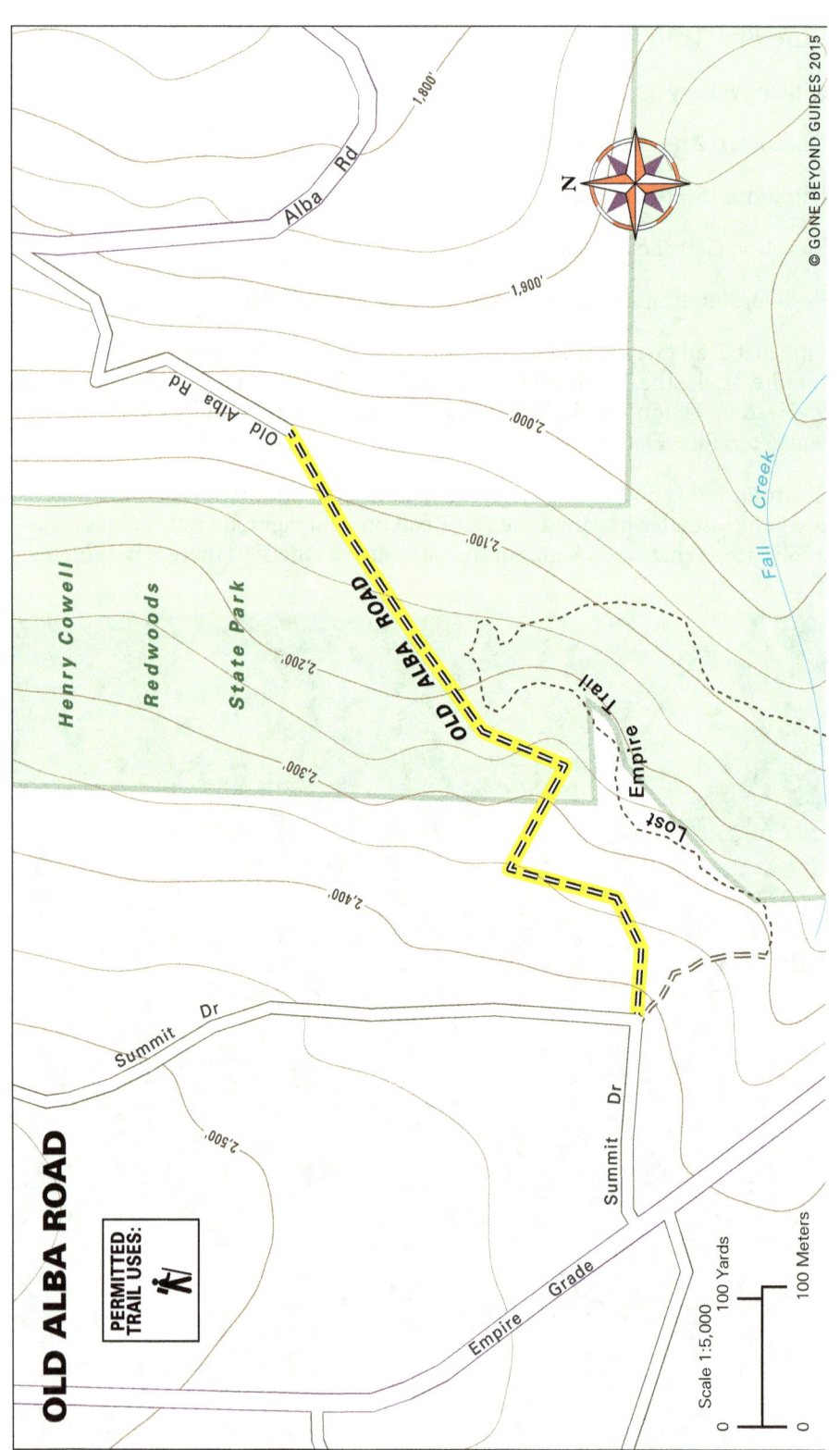

Old Alba Road

Difficulty: Easy

Distance: 0.3 miles / 0.5 km

Duration: 15 - 30 minutes

Elevation Gain/Loss: 300 feet

Best For: Experiencing an old farm road.

Old Alba Road was originally built in 1886 as a route for farmers to get into their nearest place to trade, the town of Ben Lomond. It was built from Empire Grade through Summit Road and the Old Alba Road trail. Some parts of Alba Road had a 10% grade and were so steep that horses pulling driverless wagons into Ben Lomond were reported during the period. Apparently, the driver had fallen out of the wagon seat and the horses went on to town without him. The Alba Road is also known as the Ben Lomond Grade and Alba Grade.

Old Alba Road is 6.5 miles from Felton Empire Road at Highway 9. Head up Felton Empire Road and continue right on Empire Grade until reaching Summit Road. Make a right on Summit, the trail head is just after the road turns left. This area is a residential neighborhood and parking is available for one or two cars. It is unmarked, look for the 15 mph sign as shown in the photo above.

Old Alba Road does connect to the current Alba Road, though this is not marked on the park map. The trail climbs steeply for most of the route before connecting to a locked gate and Alba Road proper.

Flora

The variety of plants in the Main and Fall Creek Units of Henry Cowell are vast. Many of plants are not native to the area and arrived starting as early as the Spanish settlers. Given that the park is bordered by a highway adds to the fact that it is an exposed park from an ecological perspective. Plants from other areas can find their way to the park and many have. Even the campground area brings a smattering of odd ball plants, such as an apple tree near one of the campsites. Even in the grove of old growth coastal redwoods there is an example of a Dawn redwood, which is native to China. In fact nearby at the Ranger Station are examples of both the Dawn and Sequoia Redwoods.

While it can be said that perhaps at this point Henry Cowell is a mix of flora at this point, there are still some areas that remain pristine and true to their original floral footprint for the most part. The park itself can be divided into four distinct habitats:

Santa Cruz Sandhills – There is an ancient sea floor in sections of Henry Cowell, leaving massive sand hills that cover much of the park near the campground. The sandy soil creates a distinct set of challenges for plants that set out to grow there. There are some species that thrive and are found only in the sandhills.

Riparian – The curvy line of the San Lorenzo River creates a habitat that cuts through the surrounding environment, creating with its abundant water a selection of plants that thrive on the river's edge.

Grassland – Smaller pockets of the park are pure grasslands and while they look to be made up of a simple set of plants, the grassland areas are rich with variety and typically the hardest to identify.

Redwoods – Finally, Henry Cowell boasts large groves of redwood and mixed evergreens. Aside from the Redwood Grove Loop, which is a grove of old growth redwoods purposefully set aside, the rest of both the Main and Fall Creek Units contain second growth forests. The entire forests were cut to provide fuel for the lime kilns, fireplaces in San Francisco and construction timber. There are some exceptions however. In a twist of fate, if a tree was deemed imperfect and difficult to cut, the tree was spared. If you see an old growth tree with its massive trunk ask yourself what it was that allowed it to not be cut down. Many are two trees with a fused base. Others have separate bases but are leaning against each other. Whatever the reason, these imperfect trees ended up being the fittest when it came to surviving to these present times.

Santa Cruz Sandhills Chaparral Plants

Bonny Doon Manzanita (*Arctostaphylos silvicola*)

Photos used with permission of laspilitas.com

Plant Community: Santa Cruz Sandhill Chaparral

Native: Yes

Description: The word manzanita was first coined by the Spanish who saw the fruits and remarked they looked like "little apples", which in Spanish is (as you may have guessed) manzanita. A true local, the Bonny Doon Manzanita is endemic to Santa Cruz County. It is listed as a shrub but can grow to 20 feet in height and has many characteristics similar to a tree. The bark is dark red and smooth to the touch. It can be particularly artful after a rain. This species is listed as an endangered "Species of Concern". This is one of the dominant native plant species within the sandhills of Santa Cruz.

Knobcone pine (*Pinus attenuata*)

Plant Community: Santa Cruz Sandhill Chaparral

Native: Yes

Description: The Knobcone pine is common from southern Oregon to Baja California and is most abundant in northern California. It prefers mild climates and dry rocky mountain soils and can be a shrub if the soil is especially poor. The leaves are needlelike as is typical for a pine and the mature bark is a dark gray red brown with flat scaly ridges.

(Sticky Monkey) Bush monkeyflower (*Mimulus aurantiacus*)

Plant Community: Santa Cruz Sandhill Chaparral

Native: Yes

Description: Also known as the Orange bush monkeyflower, this shrub is easily recognized by its deep green and sticky leaves and tubular flowers.

It thrives in many soils, wet, dry, sandy or rocky. The Monkeyflower is the host plant for the Checkerspot butterfly, which is federally threatened but not uncommon to see them on this sticky shrub. The Santa Cruz monkeyflower (var. decurtatus) is listed on the California Native Plant Society's "watch list" due to its limited habitat.

Wartleaf Ceanothus (*Ceanothus papillosus*)

Plant Community: Santa Cruz Sandhill Chaparral

Native: Yes

Description: The majority of the Ceanothus family are evergreen plants and are part of a typical diet for deer. Together, the Ceanothus family within California is commonly referred to as California Lilac.

The Wartleaf member of the Ceanothus family is endemic to California and gets its name by the unusual bumpy leaves which are long with turned under edges and lined with small hairs.

Ponderosa Pine (*Pinus ponderosa var. pacifica*)

Plant Community: Santa Cruz Sandhill Chaparral

Native: Yes

Description: This native of California and the western United States is one of the bigger and bolder pines in the Pine family. While native to the US, it is found around the world in the more temperate climates. The Ponderosa is the official state tree of Montana.

The Ponderosa Pine is best recognized from other pines by its cinnamon-red bark cracked with black crevices. To distinguish the Pacific subspecies start by looking at the number of needles per cluster. There are 4 subspecies that have up to 3, but only the Pacific and North Plateau have exactly 3. From there, best to get out the ruler you of course brought with you and compare cone scales. Pacific subspecies are wider, up to 23mm.

Bush Poppy (*Dendromecon rigida*)

Plant Community: Chaparral

Native: Yes

Description: Also known as the tree poppy, this plant can grow as a small shrub up to a small tree. It is another native of California ranging from northern Baja California through the Coast Ranges of California and as far east as the Sierra Nevada mountains. It prefers dry slopes and washes and will be one of the first plants to take root after a fire.

The evergreen leaves of the bush poppy are leathery to the touch. The satiny yellow flowers have four petals each and blooms in late winter to mid spring

Yerba Santa (*Eriodictyon californicum*)

Plant Community: Chaparral

Native: Yes

Description: This plant goes by many names, including yerba santa, mountain balm, bear weed and consumptive's weed. It is native to both California and Oregon found both in chaparral and redwood forest communities.

The leaves are sticky to the touch and are often associated with a black fungi (living in a harmless mutual relationship). The plant gives off a bitter odor that signals to animals that if it smells bad, it must taste worse, which is why most animals stay away from it. Ironically, one of the plants compounds, Eriodictyl, is by itself used in the food industry to mask bitter taste in foods.

The Papilio eurymedon butterfly is one of the few insects that use the yerba santa as part of its diet.

Bracken Fern (*Pteridium aquilinum* var. *pubescens*)

Plant Community: Chaparral, Mixed Evergreen, and Redwood

Native: Yes

Description: While the Bracken Fern is native to California, its light spores have allowed it become distributed around the world and is actually invasive in England.

The plant is easily recognized from other ferns by its hearty growth and roughly triangular fronds.

Diffuse Spineflower (*Chorizanthe diffusa*)

Plant Community: Chaparral

Native: Yes

Description: The Diffuse Spineflower can be found mainly on the central California coast. This native of California produces beautiful sprays of flowers that radiate like a firework display. The flower is white, about 3 millimeters wide and has a small yellow throat. The plant is a member of the buckwheat family.

California Rock-rose (*Helianthemum scoparium*)

Plant Community: Chaparral

Native: Yes

Description: Also known as the peak rockrose and peak rushrose, this plant is a small perennial shrub and is best spotted by its clump of green small leaves with random spray of bright yellow flowers containing five petals each.

Riparian/Riverside Plants

Boxelder (*Acer negundo* var. *californicum*)

Plant Community: Riparian/Riverside Plants

Native: Yes

Description: Also known as the California Boxelder, this relative of the maple tree is fast growing and fairly short lived, having several trunks that combine to make off trail hiking a challenge. The subspecies *californicum* has larger leaves than the main species and are velvety to the touch.

Arroyo willow (*Salix lasiolepis*)

Plant Community: Riparian/Riverside Plants

Native: Yes

Description: This is a common treelike shrub found within most of the coastal ranges throughout California. It is a deciduous plant growing up to 33 feet tall. The shoots are recognized as yellowish brown and very hairy when young. The arroyo willow flowers in the spring with yellow catkins (Dutch for "kitten" as catkins resemble a kitten's tail).

Big Leaf Maple (*Acer macrophyllum*)

Plant Community: Riparian/Riverside Plants

Native: Yes

Description: The big leaf maple is easily recognized by its large fanning leaves. Also called the Oregon Maple, this large deciduous tree prefers life near streams or moist areas. In the moister habitats they can become the dominant tree in the forest.

The big leaf maple is commercially used for its fine quality lumber. It is used mainly where wood grain relief can express itself such as furniture, stringed instruments or wood bowls. It is also possible to get maple syrup from the tree and has relatively the same sugar content as the sugar maple. That being said, it produces a sappier flavor spectrum and isn't widely used commercially, though deer and horses love the saplings.

Black Cottonwood (*Populus trichocarpa*)

Plant Community: Riparian/Riverside Plants

Native: Yes

Description: The native range of the black cottonwood covers much of western North America from Alaska to northern Baja California. It gets its name cottonwood from the hairy fruits it produces. The tree is large and is recognized by its grey bark covered with deep fissures.

Black cottonwood is used primarily for production of high quality paper, while living trees have been planted as windbreaks. The tree contains salicin, a form of natural aspirin and was used by Pacific Northwest tribes to reduce swelling, headaches and even baldness.

White Alder (*Alnus rhombifolia*)

Plant Community: Riparian/Riverside Plants

Native: Yes

Description: This medium sized deciduous tree is a native of western North America

extending into British Columbia. While listed here in the riparian ecosystem, the tree, which grows to elevations of 7900 feet is equally at home in the chaparral region of the park.

The white alder will typically grow to between 50-80 feet high and can be recognized by the compact woody catkins that resemble cones. The white alder is closely related to the red alder, with the red alder having leaves that are typically curl under towards the tip as opposed to the white alder which has leaves that are more flat. When the tree is bloom, the difference is more obvious, the catkins of one are white, the other red.

Western Sycamore (*Platanus racemosa*)

Plant Community: Riparian/Riverside Plants

Native: Yes

Description: Also known as the California sycamore and California plane tree, this California native prefers life near rivers or springs. The tree's bark is one of its most identifiable aspects. The bark is a patchwork of modern natural art, showing in patches of white, beige, browns and gray. The other key characteristics are its seed balls, which will hang from the tree in manner that is reminiscent of Dr. Seuss art.

The wood is not easy to split which limits its commercial use to butcher blocks. The plants pollen is a known allergen for some people.

Western Azalea (*Rhododendron occidentale*)

Plant Community: Riparian/Riverside Plants

Native: Yes

Description: The western azalea has been a favorite of explorers and botanists as far back as the middle of the nineteenth century. It is certainly one of the stand outs within the coastal ranges of western North America. The plant does prefer a moister environment and has a high degree of diversity in the plant's appearance. The incredibly fragrant flowers range in color from white to pink, with a splash of yellow and take an overall form of a five pointed star. The plant does grow in the serpentine soils of the Cascades and the western Sierra Nevada mountains and as far north as Oregon.

Bleeding Hearts (*Dicentra formosa*)

Plant Community: Riparian/Riverside Plants

Native: Yes

Description: This unique plant is identified by its fern like finely divided leaves that come straight from the base of the plant. Within this spray of green will pop out delicate pink, white or red heart shaped flower clusters, from which it gets its name. The flowers start blooming in mid-autumn peaking in spring.

Dog Violet (*Viola adunca*)

Plant Community: Riparian/Riverside Plants

Native: Yes

Description: One of the gems of Henry Cowell Redwoods State Park this species of violet produces a single stem from which to perch a single violet flower with deep purple veining. This is truly a beautiful flower in its simplicity and elegance. The flower actually grows throughout North America. It is also known as the sand violet and hookedspur violet.

Giant Wake Robin (*Trillium chloropetalum*)

Plant Community: Riparian/Riverside Plants

Native: Yes

Description: While the broad leaves grouped in threes alone make for a nice forest floor canopy, the western wake robin is especially beautiful in the spring when it produces dark red to white flowers in the same grouping of three. The plant is of the same genus as the trillium, the famed three petal flower that grows in the redwood ecosystem. This plant goes by many names, including the common trillium, giant trillium, sessile trillium and the giant wake robin. The term "wake robin" comes from the early spring blooms that come out before the robins return from their winter homes.

Redwood and Mixed Evergreen Forest

Tanoak (*Notholithocarpus densiflorus*)

Plant Community: Redwood and Mixed Evergreen Forest

Native: Yes

Description: The tanoak is easily spotted with its serrated elongated leaves. The tree gets its name from its tannin rich bark, which was used for tanning leather in the 18th century. While modern tanning mechanisms replaced its use in the leather industry, it is still considered for its timber, with roughly 50 million board feet of sustainable forestlands in northern California.

Madrone (*Arbutus menziesii*)

Plant Community: Redwood and Mixed Evergreen Forest

Native: Yes

Description: The madrone has a rather unique alternative name, the refrigerator tree. Since the tree does not have an external layer of bark, what is touchable is living energy producing tree, a great majority of which involves the transport of water and other nutrients up from its roots to its stems. This gives the tree a cooling effect. As noted, the madrone is easily spotted by its paper thin bark that is constantly shedding itself in brown sheets. The madrone is in decline as it depends greatly on forest fires for the germination of its seeds. With wildfires being increasingly under the control of man, the madrone has reduced opportunity to sprout new trees. Within the park, the berries of the madrone are eaten by many birds and mammals including the mule deer that will even eat the young shoots.

Douglas-fir (*Pseudotsuga menziesii*)

Plant Community: Redwood and Mixed Evergreen Forest

Native: Yes

Description: The Douglas-fir has a wide range and is contiguous from the western Cascades to the Pacific Coast Ranges down as far south as Santa Barbara County. The tree's Latin name *menziesii* comes from Archibald Menzies, a Scottish naturalist who first documented the tree on Vancouver Island in 1791. This is quite an honor for Menzies as the Douglas fir is now considered the most commercially important tree in the North American west.

The Douglas-fir's rapid growth and high yield make it a darling of the timber industry. It dries without warping and is a solid "go to" wood for dimensional lumber, timbers, pilings and plywood. It can be treated with creosote and used in outside decking, marine structures and landscaping. It is also the most popular choice for the family Christmas tree in North America.

Coast Redwood (*Sequoia sempervirens*)

Plant Community: Redwood and Mixed Evergreen Forest

Native: Yes

Description: The coastal redwood is the tallest living tree on the planet. From the same family; the giant sequoia redwood (*Sequoiadendron giganteum*), is the largest. The tallest redwood Hyperion resides in Redwood National Park and is just over 379 feet in height.

The coast redwood occupies a narrow strip of land along the Pacific coast of North America, with a range starting in Monterey County, California extending as far north as the southernmost tip of Oregon. They greatly depend on moisture from coastal fog and their small leaves have evolved to become quite adept at capturing the coastal mist for their water supply. It is not uncommon to stand in a grove of redwoods on a foggy morning and feel the cool drops of "redwood rain" as the trees capture and release the fog layer to feed their roots.

The Latin word for the tree, "sempervirens", means "everlasting" and this is not far from the truth. The trees can live to be over 2200 years old with many of the old growth stands exceeding 600 years. The trees are well adapted to survival; they are able to better withstand fires, are rich in insect repelling tannins and have an ability to literally pull water out of the air.

Perhaps the agedness of the coastal redwood is what gives it perhaps its most remarkable characteristic, majesty. Standing in a grove of the tallest living organism that has been alive for hundreds or even thousands of years brings a sense of awe and wonder to anyone who stops to ponder.

The First European Description of the Coastal Redwood

"The River of Santa Ana (Pajaro River), a very good spot for a very large mission, with a great deal of soil and water for irrigating it, and a vast amount of trees, for, besides the great many good-sized cottonwoods that there are on the river, a large range of mountains begins here having timber that is very like the pine in its leaf save that this one is not over two fingers in length; it has very sharp-pointed small cones that are not over two fingers long; the heartwood of the tree is red, a very handsome wood, nicer than cedar, so that no one knew what kind of wood it might be- we cannot tell whether it may be spruce; many said it was savin, and savin it was dubbed. There is a great number of this sort of trees here, of all sizes and thickness, most of them vastly tall, and straight like so many candles; it is a pleasure to view this blessing of timber." (Padre Juan Crespi, Portola Expedition, October 8, 1769; in Brown 2001:553).

California Bay (*Umbellularia californica*)
(aka – Pepperwood, Bay Laurel, Bay Tree, Oregon Myrtle)

Plant Community: Redwood and Mixed Evergreen Forest

Native: Yes

Description: The California bay is a hardwood tree native to the California region. The tree's aromatic leaves are similar and actually stronger than bay leaves and it may be mistaken for the bay laurel. The leaves of the California bay are smooth edged and lance shaped as are the bay laurel. However, the California bay will typically have narrower leaves and lack the crinkled margins and vein like quality of the bay laurel.

The California bay was used by many Native American tribes to cure many ailments including headaches, sore throat and clearing of the sinuses. Ironically, the purified oil of the bay laurel is well documented for inducing headaches rather than curing it, thus proving that old world remedies and science don't always see eye to eye. Both the flesh and inner kernel of the fruit was used in the Native American diet. The fruit is similar to the avocado and the large pit was roasted and eaten whole. The flavor notes of this nut include dark chocolate, coffee and burnt popcorn. The leaves are used even today in pet bedding to repel fleas.

Santa Cruz Mountain Oak (*Quercus parvula* var. *shrevei*)

Plant Community: Redwood and Mixed Evergreen Forest

Native: Yes

Description: This evergreen oak is native and highly variable, sometimes appearing as a shrub.

Poison Oak (*Toxicodendron diversilobum*)

Plant Community: All Park Ecosystems

Native: Yes

Description: There is an old adage for poison oak, "Leaves of three, leave them be." While there are several species that share the same ecosystem and characteristics of poison oak, this is a good rule of thumb as the plants toxic effects are not only irritating, they can be long lasting (up to 2-3 weeks).

Poison oak effects are actually an allergic reaction to the plants surface oil, urushiol and develop over time. There are cases where people have been repeatedly exposed to the plant and did not develop any adverse side effects. Yet with each exposure the chances of getting a rash from poison oak increase. When in an area with poison oak, it is important to minimize both exposure to the plant and any animals that are on the walk with you. Fido is immune to urushiol but the oil can easily rub off on him, passing it to you. Wash up thoroughly with soap and water if you feel you or your pet have been in contact.

Effects include severe itching along the affected area, inflammation, colorless bumps and blistering if overly scratched. In the late fall and winter, the plant loses its leaves, however the branches are still loaded with urushiol. There have been cases of campers using poison oak branches to toast marshmallows or hot dogs which resulted in hospitalization. Burning poison oak creates the highest threat as the smoke can bathe the victim's skin as well as their lungs and throat.

The plant itself is highly variable and can be a dense shrub, a tree, a vine and even a sprawling low shrub. The leaves are divided into three and are scalloped and do resemble that of true oaks.

Swordfern (*Polystichum munitum*)

Plant Community: Redwood and Mixed Evergreen Forest

Native: Yes

Description: The sword fern is a native of North America and is most abundant along the Pacific Coast. Common to ferns but very notable to the swordfern are the two rows of brown sori on the underside of the leaf frond. These spores are an ancient but still effective means of reproduction.

One interesting side note is its use for stinging nettle attacks. Simply rub the underside spores of a swordfern into the affected area to get instant relief. As the two plants typically grow together, a cure for the fiery sting should be nearby.

California Hazelnut (*Corylus cornuta* ssp. *californica*)

Plant Community: Redwood and Mixed Evergreen Forest

Native: Yes

Description: The western beaked hazel is named for its fruit which resembles a beak. Like the alders, the flowers grow in long catkins that form in the fall to be pollinated in the spring. Native Americans would encourage hazelnut growth by putting the plant under stress to grow and produce seed by lighting the surrounding area on fire.

Western Chain Fern (*Woodwardia fimbriata*)

Plant Community: Redwood and Mixed Evergreen Forest

Native: Yes

Description: The western or giant chain fern is best spotted by its long fronds, which can reach up to seven feet. It prefers coniferous forests and is a native of western North America. As with most ferns, the underside of the chain fern contain the reproductive sori spores. The sori of the chain fern are short and orderly arranged in lines which resemble a chain.

Western Trillium (*Trillium ovatum*)

Plant Community: Redwood and Mixed Evergreen Forest

Native: Yes

Description: The Pacific or western trillium stands out amongst the rich greens and browns of the redwood forest. It isn't the only flower amongst the redwoods, but it is certainly one of the largest. It stands alone as a common and pleasant sight in the canopy of the coastal redwood. The trillium has three petals, three leaves and three sepals, which is how the plant gets its name.

California Fetid Adder's Tongue (*Scoliopus bigelovii*)

Plant Community: Redwood and Mixed Evergreen Forest

Native: Yes

Description: The fetid adder's tongue is arguably the winner of any darkly beautiful plant contest. The shade of purple within the flower is darker than a zinfandel, with deliberate strips of pure white as a contrasting offset. This lily has lance shaped sepals that not only strike at the air, but do so again with that same deathly dark shade of purple.

The fetid adder's tongue name betrays two of the plants characteristics. This lily blooms early, in January to February timeframe. The flowers, which appear in groups of three, give off a fowl unpleasant scent, hence the fetid part. As the flower dies off, only the large leaves remain, sticking out of the ground like the tongue of an adder snake.

Both the odor and the near ultraviolet deep maroon of the flower are thought to act as an attractant to fungus gnats that help pollinate the plant. This lily is found primarily in the understory of old growth redwood forests.

Western Hound's Tongue (*Cynoglossum grande*)

Plant Community: Redwood and Mixed Evergreen Forest

Native: Yes

Description: The distribution of the Western Hound's Tongue extends across most of western North America, preferring shady woodland areas, but can also be found in chaparral ecosystems. It is a perennial herb whose leaves sprout directly from the ground. The flower is a cluster of five lobed flowerets that range from bright to deep blue.

Milkmaids (*Cardamine californica*)

Plant Community: Redwood and Mixed Evergreen Forest

Native: Yes

Description: It hard not to fall in love with the milkmaids. They are simple, pleasant clean white and light pink flowers from the Mustard family (Brassicaceae). It native to western North America and is an early bloomer, coming out from January to May. The flower has a mechanism to protect its precious pollen by closing it petals with the setting of the sun and will even droop its stem downward in a rain.

Redwood Sorrel (*Oxalis oregana*)

Plant Community: Redwood and Mixed Evergreen Forest

Native: Yes

Description: It is easy to notice the delicate understory of the redwood sorrel, looking like heart shaped three leaf clovers, they provide an elfin quality and certainly add to the serenity of any walk through the redwoods.

They will spread across a few square feet or more, shutting out other species. They have adapted very well to the often dark canopy of the coastal redwood and require only 1/200th of full sunlight. To this, if direct sunlight does hit them, they will fold their leaves downward and then reopen them when the shade returns. The observant hiker can witness this physical movement with the naked eye as they will return to their original outstretched shape in just a few minutes.

Redwood sorrel is mildly toxic to humans, containing oxalic acid, which is a known component in the creation of kidney stones and joint pain.

Grassland/Meadow

Coyote Brush (*Baccharis pilularis* ssp. *consanguinea*)

Plant Community: All Park Ecosystems

Native: Yes

Description: This shrub is also called chaparral broom and bush baccharis. Another native, it is a hardy plant that is considered a secondary pioneer plant in the chaparral communities. As a result, it is an indicator of a more established ecosystem that has not undergone a fire or significant grazing. The establishment of the coyote brush helps pave the way for other native species such as the California bay and coastal live oak, which will eventually dominate and replace the shrub as the ecosystem matures in the absence of fire or grazing.

Blackberry (*Rubus ursinus*)

Plant Community: Redwood and Mixed Evergreen Forest

Native: Yes

Description: The blackberry is similar to the Himalayan blackberry and can be distinguished by having a smaller fruit but most notably the flower's petals are narrow compared to the Himalayan blackberry. Alternate names for this species include California blackberry, Douglas blackberry and Pacific dewberry.

Oats (*Avena* sp.)

Plant Community: Prairie Grasslands, Chaparral

Native: No

Description: Before you read this and think you can harvest the oats in Henry Cowell Redwoods State Park, it's worth noting that these are wild oats and are hard to harvest. The oats in your oatmeal are known as the common oat and produce a far greater yield than the ones the park can provide. Wild oats are actually invasive to cereal crops and since both varieties are grasses and similar, eradication is difficult. That being said, if you do find yourself stuck in Henry Cowell for an extended period of time due to a zombie apocalypse or other similar scenario, the wild oat versions are edible.

The problematic nature of wild oats in the production of grains is long standing and the term "Sowing wild oats" was first noted in 1542 by Thomas Beccon, a Protestant clergyman in Norfolk, England. Beccon used it in reference to an unprofitable activity since trying to weed out wild oats in a field of common oats is a meticulous task. Oat grains then gained the reputation as an "invigorating" food. Over time the meaning of "sowing wild oats" changed to indicate a sexual liaison ending in an out of wedlock child.

Beardless Wild Rye (*Elymus triticoides*)

Plant Community: Prairie Grasslands, Chaparral

Native: Yes

Description: Considered one of the native grasses of California, this is true species of wild rye. It is found across western North America and loves a moist habitat forming a solid root system. The roots will actually trap soil such that the grass can live right up to the water's edge. This property allows it to be used to stabilize waterways and other restoration projects where holding the soil in place is needed.

California Poppy (*Eschscholzia californica*)

Plant Community: Prairie Grasslands, Chaparral

Native: Yes

Description: If you grew up in California, you learn at a very early age two things about the California poppy; they are the State Flower and most importantly, you will be fined $500 for each one you pick. As a boy, this was a really big deterrent to picking the flower and picking a dozen for mom at six grand was simply out of the question.

On it being the State flower the answer is yes and it has been since 1903 (April 6th is California Poppy Day). In terms of getting fined, it is illegal to pick any flower, shrub, tree, etc. if it is on State land, such as Henry Cowell Redwoods State Park. If you grow them around your home however, pick as many as you like.

Other things to know about the California poppy. They don't contain any opium but contain a different class of alkaloids which have been studied as an antidepressant. The results so far are that the effect is too mild to be an effective treatment. The poppy flower will close at night.

Common Madia (*Madia elegans*)

Plant Community: Prairie Grasslands, Chaparral

Native: Yes

Description: This bright lemon yellow daisy like flower is native to western North America. The flower color can also vary to lemon with a center of a different color of white or maroon. The flower has a spicy and fragrant scent when it opens up in the late afternoon through the night. During the day the flower will close up. Its fruit have been collected by some Native Americans and were ground into a flour, though it is not known if the Ohlone Indians practiced this method. The plant subspecies are also known as tarweeds.

Padre's Shooting Star (*Primula clevelandii* var. *gracillis*)

Plant Community: Prairie Grasslands, Chaparral

Native: Yes

Description: The Padre's Shooting Star is a deciduous plant that blooms during the rainy season and dies back as the season becomes warmer and drier. The stem can grow up to a foot tall, supporting magenta, purple or white flowers. It is a native of California and Baja.

This flower is part of the genus Primula, which are identified by having their petals thrust back exposing the reproductive bits making them easy for bees and other insects to pollinate. Bees will even utilize a special method for collecting pollen on these types of flowers. They will grab the petals and gather pollen by buzzing their wings, which vibrates the flower into releasing pollen.

Wavy Leaf Soap Plant (*Chlorogalum pomeridianum* var. *pomeridianum*)

Plant Community: Prairie Grasslands, Chaparral

Native: Yes

Description: The wavy soap plant grows from a bulb and is found in California and southwestern Oregon. The leaves are somewhat wavy, hence its name, but this isn't always evident. The flowers, which are usually white or white with a bit of green or purple, open in late afternoon and stay open throughout the night, closing in the morning.

Purple Owl's Clover (*Castilleja exserta* ssp. *exserta*)

Plant Community: Prairie Grasslands, Chaparral

Native: Yes

Description: This flower is native to the Southwestern United States and is an annual about 1 foot tall. The plant is considered a hemiparasitic plant, which means it lives off the nutrients of other plants and photosynthesis. Hemiparasites have various ways of living off their host plant. In the case of the purple owl's clover, the plant will inject the host plant's roots with a parasitic fungus that break down the root's cell walls and allow for easier movement of organic carbon from the host back to the plant via the fungus. This relationship between host, fungus and parasite plant is quite interesting and complex. Studies have indicated that perhaps the host plant actually acts under the control of the fungus, abiding by the signals given to it by the invader.

Vetch spp. (*Vicia* spp.)

Plant Community: Prairie Grasslands, Chaparral

Native: Yes

Description: The Vicia is a member of the pea or legume family and is known as one of the first cultivated seed crops. It has been recorded to have been grown in the Near East a very long 9,500 years ago. It can be made into a bread meal and was used as a crop of last resort or amongst the impoverished.

Over the centuries, vetches became more important as a forage plant for cows and sheep. In current times, it has been found to be toxic to humans if eaten in quantity and not recommended as a staple for even cows and other rudiments. That being said, it is a typical food plant of the caterpillars of many moths and butterflies so its fate as an edible food hasn't completely disappeared after all these years. It is native on every continent expect Antarctica.

Cow Parsnip (*Heracleum maximum*)

Plant Community: Prairie Grasslands, Chaparral

Native: Yes

Description: This very common plant is found throughout North America with the exception of the Gulf Coast. It can become quite large, up to 7 feet tall. It genus name *Heracleum* is a reference to the flower's huge size. The cow parsnip is easy to recognize due both to its large size and it unique clusters of white flowers which collectively look like a group of white inverted umbrellas.

The plant has good reputation as a medicine and food amongst the Native Americans. You can peel the outer skin of young plants and eat them. You can grind them up and apply them as poultices for bruises. You can dry the stem and use them as straws. Potentially the most relevant use is that the flowers can be rubbed on the skin to repel mosquitoes and flies.

Fauna

The amount of wildlife in Cowell is stunning in both number and variety. There are numerous rodents, insectivores, rabbits, deer, foxes, coyotes, bobcats and mountain lions all coexisting in the park.

Trout (Salmonidae)

Coastal Rainbow Trout
(*Oncorhynchus mykiss irideus*, aka Steelhead Trout)

Conservation Status: Threatened or Endangered depending on subspecies

Description: The Salmonidae family of fish include salmon, trout, chars and graylings. They spawn in fresh water and then spend most of their lives in the ocean, returning to the rivers from which they were born only to reproduce. This lifecycle is referred to as anadromous. Juvenile steelhead will live up to three years in the river before heading to sea.

On returning to the rivers to spawn, the adult steelhead are faced with multiple environmental factors, including dams, water pollution and general urbanization of the watershed. These become impediments towards spawning and are major factors in the overall decline of the species.

While steelhead and salmon species in the San Lorenzo River are not immune to these pressures, they are present. Catch and release fishing is permitted for both from December to February as governed by the California Department of Fish and Game. Check first on the exact fishing season, a fishing permit is required.

Salamanders (Caudata)

Rough-skinned newts (*Taricha granulosa*)

Conservation Status: Least Concern

Description: The Rough skinned newt is fairly common especially around shores of still ponds and moist areas. They are fairly slow moving and can be quite docile. While this makes them easy to catch don't let their benign appearance fool you. These guys exude a toxin called tarichatoxin that can cause paralysis and even death. Respect the newt.

Tarichatoxin is the same toxin found in pufferfish, some toads, certain angelfish and several sea stars. The first recorded poisoning due to tarichatoxin was from the crew of Captain James Cook in 1774. Apparently the crew dined on some pufferfish and then fed the scraps to their pigs. The crew experienced numbness and shortness of breath while all the pigs, who ate the more toxic body parts, were found dead the following morning. Tarichatoxin is the main ingredient used in Voodoo magic to turn humans into "zombies".

Symptoms start with a slight numbness of the lips and tongue followed by paralysis of facial muscles. Second stage symptoms are noticed as increasing paralysis. As there is no known antivenom, treatment involves stomach pumping, activated charcoal ingestion and life support.

There was a case of one man who on a dare ate a newt and died shortly thereafter. The toxin must be ingested so if you do accidently touch one and then read this, wash your hands immediately and it goes without saying, don't put your hands in your mouth. If contact has been made and in doubt, seek medical attention.

Now that you have a bit more respect for the newt, here's a brief synopsis for this rather cute little water creature. They are carnivorous, eating insects, spiders and amphibians. They have a strong sense of smell and are able to find concentrations of hatchling tadpoles. They have also been observed stalking their prey.

They will migrate to breeding waters such as still ponds beginning in October creating at times amazing amounts of newts in a single body of water (up to 5000 per hectare have been reported). Females will lay eggs which will develop into a pole, metamorphosing by the next summer into juveniles who then become terrestrial and migrate some distance away. They reach sexual maturity after 2-4 years.

Slugs (Gastropoda)

Banana slug (*Ariolamax californicus, Ariolimax columbianus and Ariolimax dolichophallus*)

Conservation Status: Least Concern

Description: The slender banana slug is indeed the official mascot of the UC Santa Cruz "Slugs" and so a State Park that harbors them this close to the campus deserves a nod to this slimy little fellow. They are typically bright yellow and like all members of the mollusk family do not do well if dehydrated. The banana slug deals with this by producing a slime that can absorb water in incredible quantities, up to 100 times its initial volume. Trying to wash the slime off of one's hands will demonstrate this as it is very difficult to remove. It's best to wipe the slime off with a dry towel or rub your hands together until the slime rolls up into a rubber cement like ball.

Species include the California, Pacific and slender banana slug. Some slugs do develop black spots to the point of looking almost entirely black. It is the second largest terrestrial slug in the world growing to over 9 inches in length. A close look will reveal two sets of tentacles. The larger ones on top detect light and movement while the lower ones detect chemicals. They live to eat leaves, animal droppings and other dead plant material and turn the food into rich organic matter.

Opossums (Didelphidae)

Virginia Opossum (*Didelphis virginiana*)

Conservation Status: Least Concern

Description:

"My love is an opossum, unexpected,

oddly shaped, close to the ground

and somehow resolute, certain of itself,

and you." – quote from Richard Beben's "What the Heart Weighs"

Opossums make up the largest order of marsupials in the Western Hemisphere and the Virginia opossum, found here in Cowell was the first animal to be named an opossum, back in 1610. If you caught that opossums are marsupials and thought kangaroo, you'd be correct; they do come from the same Infraclass and share in the same "baby in a pouch" characteristics.

Opossums are about the size of a large house cat, nocturnal, solitary and great opportunists. It is not terribly shy within the range of humans, using the cover of night to top over garbage cans and eat pet food. Opossums actually have opposable "thumbs" on their back feet as well as 50 teeth, the most of any mammal in North America.

Opossums are omnivorous, which adds to their opportunistic qualities, which is to say, they aren't picky in what they eat, including known cases of eating each other. They live about two years, which is typical for marsupials. The opossums reproduce similar to other mammals however the young are born at a very early stage. The young is then faced with its first challenge, to find its way into the pouch (marsupium) for food and all the comforts of mom. They make the pouch their home between 70-125 days before getting the boot. Once they do leave the pouch, one can image the young getting a suitcase and some general advice on how to make it on their own in the world however this particular point is well debated and is considered by some as being completely fictional whimsy on behalf of the author.

The notion that opossums will play dead is not a myth. If threatened, they will "play possum", mimicking the appearance and even smell of a dead or dying animal. What is interesting is that the opossum actually faints, presumably out of fear and does not consciously pretend to be dead. When their brain triggers the physiological response, the lips will draw back barring the teeth, saliva will form around the mouth, the eyes will close and a foul smell will exude from their nether regions. One can actually pick them up by their stiff, curled tail. They will remain unconscious for 40 minutes to up to 4 hours.

Insectivores (Insectivora)

Trowbridge's Shrew (*Sorex trowbridgii*)

Conservation Status: Least Concern

Description: Shrew's in general are not mice, nor are they rodents, though the Trowbridge shrew does look like a mouse with a long nose. What makes them different is shrews have sharp spike like teeth whereas the mouse has more blunt gnawing teeth. These sharper teeth are used primarily for catching insects, which puts the shrew in the category of insectivore (insect eater).

Shrews have horrible eyesight but make up for it with a great sense of smell and hearing. They prefer insects and worms but will augment their diets with seeds and nuts as well. They are very active, always looking for food to satisfy their extremely high metabolisms.

While the shrew does not hibernate, it does enter into a state of torpor which can result in a winter weight loss of up to 50% of their body weight.

While the Trowbridge shrew itself is not known to do this, some shrews can echolocate (use sound to navigate by). The Trowbridge shrew is venomous, which is very unusual for a mammal. It carries its venom through grooves in its teeth which are lethal enough to kill 200 mice. It is rare for humans to encounter the bite of the shrew.

Perhaps the biggest claim to fame of the shrew is that it's brain is 10% of its body mass, the greatest of any mammal, including us, who have a mere 2.5% brain to body mass ratio. Fortunately, it appears that this ratio is not an indication of actual intelligence. If it were, we would most certainly be ruled by echo-locating shrews with vampire like qualities.

Shrew-mole (*Neurotrichus gibbsii*)

Conservation Status: Least Concern

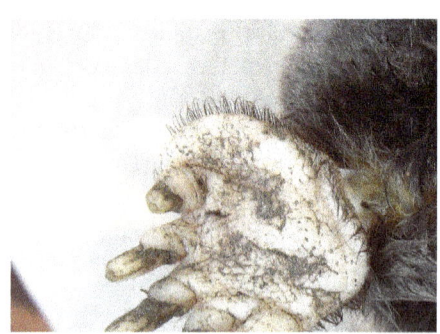

Description: This little guy is the smallest North American mole. It has the long nosed characteristics of the shrew, which gives it half its name. Moles however are subterranean purists, preferring life in the underground. They are highly adapted to living in holes to the point that they have a higher tolerance for carbon dioxide than other mammals. They also have an extra thumb (which would give them the ability to give four thumbs up if they were able to rate movies). The extra thumb and lack of sharp needle like teeth are what separate them from the true shrew.

Moles love earthworms and other insect like creatures they can find in the dirt. They, like shrews will augment their diet with nuts. Also like shrews, they have a venom in their saliva which allows them to paralyze and stockpile earthworms, creating underground larders. Researchers have found such larders with over a thousand earthworms in them. The mole will actually pull an earthworm through their paws to squeeze out the collected earth in the worms belly prior to eating it.

Broad-footed Mole (*Scapanus latimanus*)

Conservation Status: Least Concern

Description: The Broad Footed Mole is similar to other moles and are distinguished by having forefeet that are almost as wide as they are long. Other than that, they are very much like the Shrew-Mole.

Bats (Chiroptera)

Townsend's Big-eared Bat (*Corynorhinus townsendii*)

Photo: Dave Bunnell

Conservation Status: Least Concern

Description: For most people, bats are cool and scary all at the same time. There is tremendous wonder if you ever see one flying around with near insect like flight precision and tremendous creepiness if you've ever been in a small cave with a bunch of them zipping around your head.

The Townsend's big-eared bat gets its name due to its extremely long, flexible ears. Townsend's bat has a uniform body color that is a wood brown, with dark brown wings. They hibernate in the winter, where they huddle in tight clusters to keep themselves warm. Unlike the deep hibernation of bears, the Townsend's bat will wake up frequently to find a warmer part of the pack.

The Townsend's big-eared bat can live up to 16 years and they mate in the fall where the courtship falls with the male. Like humans, the pups are born pink, naked and helpless. For food, they hunt at night using echolocation to find their prey. Their diet is made up of small insects, including moths and flies.

Hares and Rabbits (Lagomorpha)

Brush Rabbit (*Sylvilagus bachmani*)

Conservation Status: Least Concern

Description: The brush rabbit or western brush rabbit is one of the cottontail rabbits found in the coastal regions of the west. They hop around from the Columbia River in Oregon to Cabo San Lucas down in Baja, California and as far east as the Sierras.

The brush rabbit is aptly named as it prefers the cover of brush, even in urban areas, as its habitation area. It feeds mainly on grasses, especially clover, which it finds in patches within the brush or in the fringe around it.

Ecologically, the brush rabbit is a big part of the food chain, being prey for cougars, coyotes, foxes and even raptors and snakes. They use brush cover and when in a pinch will stand in a statue like pose in hopes to blend into their surroundings.

The old adage about rabbits is true for the Brush rabbit. It does mate year round and goes through the gestation process in a short 22 days. A Brush rabbit can have up to five litters a year with one to seven young born per litter.

Audubon's Cottontail (*Sylvilagus audubonii*)

Conservation Status: Least Concern

Description: The Audubon's or desert cottontail is similar and as common as the brush rabbit. To tell them apart, easiest is by the ears; Audubon's cottontail has the bigger ones. (The black-tailed jackrabbit also has big ears, but lacks the cottontail). Other than that there are a lot of similarities between the two rabbits. They both eat grasses, reproduce like bunnies and are a rich source of food amongst the predator types. The desert cottontail does have a range that extends much farther east. While the brush rabbit ranges as far east as the Sierra foothills, the desert cottontail lives as far as central Nevada.

The two rabbits share a lot more than diet and turf. Both were first scientifically recognized by two naturalists of the 1800's. Reverend John Bachman and John James Audubon spent a number of months travelling together and sharing in their knowledge and passion for recording nature. Together they wrote and illustrated a monumental publication on mammals called Viviparous Quadrupeds of North America. This book gave Americans of the mid-19th century their first real look at mammals within North America including many that are in Henry Cowell. The book became a go to standard for scholars and armchair naturalists and is today a benchmark in what was alive then and is extinct now.

By now you are probably saying, this is great and all, but how does this apply to brush and desert rabbits? Well, given the similarities of these two cottontails, each naturalist, Bachman and Audubon, gave themselves some due credit when naming them. The brush rabbit's Latin name is *Sylvilagus bachmani* while the desert rabbit is *Sylvilagus audubonii*. I imagine they figured by tying their name to a mammal that reproduces so well, their legacy would be sure to live on.

Black-tailed Jackrabbit (*Lepus californicus*)

Conservation Status: Least Concern

Description: The black-tailed jackrabbit is not a rabbit, nope, it is a hare. So what's a hare then? Well, it's a fast moving rabbit. (At this point, true zoologist readers are cringing, but hey, it's kinda true you guys). Hares have longer legs and are adapted to run up to an amazing 45 mph. If it hops, rabbit. If it runs at "I'm outta here" speeds, hare.

The black-tailed jackrabbit is the third largest of the North American hares and occupies mixed shrub-grassland terrains. They have a much larger range then the cottontails, found as far east as Missouri and deeper south into south central Mexico. They do not extend into Canada.

The male black-tailed jackrabbit, with its creamy white underside and dark buff fur, reaches sexual maturity at 7 months. Females usually start breeding in their second year. Gestation is between 41 to 47 days giving litter sizes of 2-7 leverets (baby hares).

It is described in the desert rabbit section that naturalists Bachman and Audubon had a big hand in the naming of both the brush and desert rabbit. They also coined the term jack rabbit. As the hare has ears resembling the donkey, and as wild donkeys went by the term "jack" (short for jackass), they arrived at the name jackrabbit.

Rodents (Rodentia)

Merriam's Chipmunk (*Tamias merriami*)

Conservation Status: Least Concern

Description: Merriam's chipmunk is one of the cuter members of the rodent family. They live below 8900 feet throughout most of central and southern California as well as northern Baja California. They build nests in logs, stumps, snags and burrows within heavy brush for cover. They are entirely herbivorous, eating acorns, seeds and other nuts. They do cache food for later use and do hibernate.

California Ground Squirrel (*Spermophilus beecheyi*)

Conservation Status: Least Concern

Description: The California ground squirrel is found everywhere in the western United States and into Baja California to the south and Washington to the north. The California ground squirrel lives in burrows that it excavates. While they will locate their burrows very close to human areas, they do not venture far from the safe haven in the ground they've created. Most of their life is spent within 80 feet of their burrow. While California ground squirrels in colder regions will hibernate, the ones at Cowell are active year round.

The biggest predators of the squirrel are rattlesnakes but they are also the favorites of hawks, eagles, raccoons and foxes. The California ground squirrel has been known to eat the skins shed by rattlesnakes to disguise their scent and will swish their tail rapidly to give the impression of a larger heat signature to the rattlesnake, who "sees" with its infra red viewing pit organs.

Western gray squirrel (*Sciurus griseus*)

Conservation Status: Least Concern

Description: The Western gray squirrel is a shy tree dweller and will give high pitched hoarse barking call if it feels threatened. Like the California ground squirrel, they are well adapted to areas that humans frequent. The California ground squirrel and the western gray squirrel both compete for the same resources.

Botta's Pocket Gopher (*Thomomys bottae*)

Conservation Status: Least Concern

Description: These stocky rodents have large check pouches, which is where the term "pocket" is derived from. Botta's pocket gopher is considered a "true" gopher as it largely uses burrowing both for creating a home and for feeding.

The Botta's gopher is highly adaptable, able to burrow in a wide array of soils, from clays to sands and from dry deserts to high altitude meadows. They spend about 90% of their life underground, eating roots of plants it finds in the over 450 feet of tunnels it will create.

The pocket gopher in general is both a pest in urban areas and a benefit in their ability to aerate the soil. For farmers of alfalfa and other grasses, they are of special concern as they have been shown to reduce the productivity of the crops by up to 50%. They are amongst the diets of coyotes, snakes, bobcats, hawks and owls.

Both the common and Latin name of the Botta pocket gopher is a nod to world explorer, archeologist and naturalist Paul-Emile Botta. The Frenchman Botta was selected as the naturalist for a French financed voyage around the world. He left from the northern city of Le Havre, France and sailed around the Cape Horn in 1826 stopping for some time in the then called "Alta California" where he did some early work in cataloguing mammals of the area. After three years and stops in Hawaii and China, Botta and the crew of the Le Heros returned safe and sound to the same port from which their travels began.

Bad Gopher Jokes

Knock Knock

Who's there!

Gopher!

Gopher who!

Gopher a long walk off a short pier! Knock Knock

Who's there!

Gopher!

Gopher who!

Gopher your gun, Sheriff! Knock Knock

Who's there!

Gopher!

Gopher who!

Gopher broke!

California Pocket Mouse (*Chaetodipus californicus*)

Conservation Status: Least Concern

Description: Found from San Francisco down to the San Diego border and east to the Sierras, this little guy is a native Californian. It is quite common amongst coast scrub, chaparral, grassland and evergreen forests and is thus found in every region within Henry Cowell. It feeds primarily on grass seeds and the occasional insect that it can capture on the ground.

The California pocket mouse is a nocturnal animal and will sleep during the day in its burrow, venturing out at night to feed. It is preyed upon by coyotes, bobcats, owls and snakes. Like the Botta's pocket gopher, the pocket mouse gets its name by storing food in its cheek pouches.

Deer Mouse (*Peromyscus maniculatus*)

Conservation Status: Least Concern

Description: The deer mouse has a broad range, from Alaska to South America. Most deer mice nest high in hollows of trees and are generally nocturnal. They are quite adaptable and are found in a vast array of ecological communities, including grasslands, chaparral and forests.

Deer mice have been a cause for concern lately as they are a vector of the hantavirus. Almost all human cases of the hantavirus have been as a result of contact with rodent excrement and the deer mouse has been documented as a host of the virus. It is not understood why the deer Mouse and not all rodents act as carriers.

Hantavirus itself gets its name from the Hantan River in South Korea where it was first discovered in the late 1970's. The hantaviruses are a relatively new genus. The first outbreak occurred amongst several thousand United Nation soldiers stationed in Korea during the Korean War. It would take 25 years to discover the cause of that outbreak. In 1993 another outbreak was recorded in the southwestern United States and has spread into the Sierras including Yosemite National Park where eight new cases and three deaths were confirmed in August 2012.

Given the viruses' recent existence, our ability to defend its onslaught is equally new. Symptoms can become quite severe and even lead to death. For most the virus gives symptoms similar to a bad flu. It will incubate within an infected human for two to four weeks before displaying the typical flu like symptoms of fever, chills, nausea and back pain.

While the flu (called HFRS) is debilitating in and of itself, a patient with HFRS is at risk to actually have Hantavirus Pulmonary Syndrome (HPS). While the symptoms are almost indistinguishable at first, HPS can lead to cardiovascular shock and is often fatal. The good news is getting HPS itself is rare, the bad news is that it is fatal in 60% of the cases. This is what gives alarm to the medical community since the early symptoms of more typical flu viruses, Hanta flu (HFRS) and the potentially fatal HPS are very similar. If you suspect you have either, it's best to seek medical attention.

Dusky-Footed Woodrat (*Neotoma fuscipes*)

Conservation Status: Least Concern

Description: Another nocturnal rodent, the dusky-footed woodrat is commonly referred to as a packrat. This is because it is known to build large domed dens that can reach several feet high. The dens are near fortresses, being able to fend off the onslaught by a coyote or other predator who will give up before reaching their prey. They look very similar to the infamous *Rattus rattus*, (the common black rat) and are distinguished from them by larger eyes and ears and furred tail.

It has been observed that the dusky-footed woodrat will intentionally place California bay leaves around the edges of their nest. Biologists believe that somehow the Woodrat made the connection that the volatile oils in the Bay leaves, which are toxic to flea larvae, would help them control fleas in their nests.

Black Rat (*Rattus rattus*)

Conservation Status: Least Concern

Description: The Bblack rat is a world traveler. Believed to have originated in India, they then spread to Egypt and throughout the Roman Empire, reaching England around the 1st century. With the advent of nautical voyages, the black rat was spread from Europe to the rest of the world.

Given that their populations can explode and the fact that they have no problem living in urban areas, the black rat has figured prominently and negatively throughout history. Perhaps their biggest claim to fame is in being tied to the Black Death, which killed nearly a quarter of the world's population, roughly 100 million people at that time, though some estimates double that figure. The death rate in some countries, like Iraq, Iran and Syria was almost a third of the population. Forty percent of Egypt's population was reduced and an astounding 50% of Paris citizens perished because of it. Occurring in the 14th century, it is considered one of the most devastating pandemics in human history.

Art of the Black Plague Period

It took Europe nearly 150 years to recover from the plague and had profound religious, social and economic effects that dramatically changed the course of European history. It led to religious persecution, targeted mostly at the Jewish population who were blamed for the crisis.

The black rat is a carrier not only for the bubonic plaque, but typhus, toxoplasmosis and trichinosis. It is a complex pest and difficult to control due to its high intelligence and extreme adaptability.

California Vole (*Microtus californicus*)

Conservation Status: Least Concern

Description: A vole is a small rodent that while resembling a mouse, has a stouter body, rounded head, and a shorter, hairy tail. The California vole is one of 155 species of the vole family. They reach sexual maturity in just one month and can have up to 10 litters per year. Under the right ecological conditions, they have achieved exponential growth. A single pregnant vole can produce more than a hundred active voles in less than a year. Given a normal ecosystem, their knack for creating lots of offspring is offset by their many predators, including hawks, raccoons and even house cats.

Carnivores (Carnivora)

Coyote (*Canis latrans*)

Conservation Status: Least Concern

"Whenever the pressure of our complex city life thins my blood and numbs my brain, I seek relief in the trail; and when I hear the coyote wailing to the yellow dawn, my cares fall from me - I am happy." – Hamlin Garland.

Description: Despite being extensively hunted, the coyote is one of the few mammals that have increased their range of habitation, originally the western half of North America and now the entire United States and Canada. This may be in part to the equally extensive hunting of wolves and their unique ability to co-exist in urban and suburban areas. The extent that they do coexist is surprising. One seven year study found there were up to 2,000 coyotes living in the greater Chicago area. Their adaptation is almost ninja like as while they adapted well to living within densely populated urban environments, they do so in a manner that is completely hidden from the humans they live amongst. The study also found that urban coyotes outlived their wilderness counterparts.

Outside of urban areas, coyotes are a big problem for ranchers of sheep, goat and cattle. According to the 2004 National Agricultural Statistics Service, coyotes were responsible for over 60% of sheep deaths in that year, some 134,000 sheep. As a result of the uneasy relationship in the suburban environments, they are actively hunted. The U.S. government routinely traps, shoots or poisons some 90,000 coyotes that range within livestock areas.

The coyote is a species of canine and primarily hunt in pairs or occasionally in larger groups. Typical packs are made of six closely related adults, juveniles and young. They live about 10 years in the wild but up to 18 in captivity.

The calls of a coyote are amongst the most awe inspiring animal sounds in nature. Typically a series of howls, yips, yelps and barks, the coyote call is a chorus of wilderness song, usually cutting the stark silence of the night. The calls echo amongst the hillsides and fills the land for miles with their series of howls and yips, dropping to some final notes and then as quickly as it began, the calls end.

Coyotes are prevalent in Native American folklore, appearing as prominent figures within creation myths at the beginning of time and as tricksters and/or heroes in current times. Whether seen as clever tricksters or a creature able to achieve the impossible, the coyote is well respected.

Gray Fox (*Urocyon cinereoargenteus*)

Conservation Status: Least Concern

Description: The gray fox has been with us for over 3.6 million years according to fossil evidence found in Arizona. Given the dramatic and complete changes in the environments in which it lived, through ice ages, jungle like conditions and present day climes, this is a pretty amazing statement.

The gray fox is nocturnal, monogamous and comes from the same family as coyotes and dogs. They are omnivorous and prefer to hunt alone. They are fairly adept at making a diet of brush and jackrabbits, as well as voles and other rodents. In desert areas where a meat diet is infrequent, the gray fox will adapt to insects and fruits for sustenance. Kits (young foxes) will begin to hunt as early as three months and can hunt on their own at four months. Once the kits reach sexual maturity, they will leave home, venturing on their own to start the cycle anew.

Raccoon (*Procyon lotor*)

Conservation Status: Least Concern

Description: Raccoons started life in deciduous and mixed forests but with the advent of humans, they have adapted to live amongst us. Their range extends throughout North America and beyond to Europe, Russia and even Japan. Raccoons are increasing in urban areas and exhibit less fear around humans than other mammals. Hunting and getting caught in traffic are the two most common causes of death. It has been found in areas where hunting is common as an eradication method, the raccoons adaptability extends to a higher rate of reproduction to compensate.

Raccoons are one of the smarter mammals that do live among and around us. A study done in 1908 by H. B. Davis found raccoons could open 11 of 13 complex locks he set out for them in fewer than 10 tries. Further studies have shown that raccoons are not only able to understand abstract principles, but could do so as quickly as a Rhesus monkey and could retain the memory of what they learned for three years.

Raccoons are nocturnal and omnivorous, eating a variety of plants, insects, worms, and easily caught fish and bird eggs. Many have observed raccoons washing their meals before eating; however it is not completely certain to scientists as to why they do this.

Raccoons are known carriers of rabies and care should be taken when around them, especially those that do not show fear of humans. That being said, with rabies vaccination policies and awareness, there has only been one documented human fatality due the transmission of rabies from a raccoon bite.

Long-tailed Weasel (*Mustela frenata*)

Conservation Status: Least Concern

Description: The long-tailed weasel is a member of the Mustelidae family, which make up a group of small active predators that are long, slender and have short legs. The long-tailed weasel is the largest of this family. They are found throughout North America and as far south as northern South America, living in rocky dens or abandoned burrows.

The long-tailed weasel will feed on animals much larger than themselves, including rabbits. Their technique is to strike in rapid fashion, biting any part of the body they can grab ahold of, climbing onto the body and digging in with their feet will continue to attack until they can inflict a lethal bite to the neck.

For night identification, the weasel's eyes will glow a bright emerald green if caught in the beam of a flashlight. During the day, their long slender body covered in an auburn brown fur makes the weasel easy to spot. The other distinction is the black tip of their tail.

Striped Skunk (*Mephitis mephitis*)

Conservation Status: Least Concern

Description: Oh, the beloved skunk, one of the few animals that invoke the question, "What's that smell?" on forest drives. The skunk is widespread throughout the United States and Canada and is one of the most recognized mammals with its black fur with double white stripe. It prefers ecosystems of woodlands, grasslands and agricultural areas.

Skunks are omnivorous, eating mainly insects but also earthworms and even honeybees. They will eat small animals such as frogs and voles as well as berries and other wild fruit. In urban areas, they can become a problem for pet owners who leave food out for the cat or dog. They have also been known to dig up lawns looking for grubs and worms. Skunks typically hunt during twilight hours of dusk and dawn, retiring to its burrow during the day.

As to who preys on the skunk, most of the typical predators don't due to the skunk's ability to fend for itself using its foul smell. The noted exception to this is the great horned owl, which lacks a sense of smell.

The widely known defense mechanism of the skunk is its ability to spray a foul smell from its anal glands. This chemical, a mixture of sulfur containing chemicals collectively called mercaptans, produce a highly offensive smell that is unique but has similar qualities to rotten eggs and burnt rubber. It is powerful enough to ward off bears and can cause skin irritation, temporary blindness and can even permanently stain house paint. The skunk can aim and disperse the chemical with a high degree of accuracy up to 10 feet. It is detectable by the human nose for up to a mile radius from where it was dispersed.

That being said, skunks will use this weapon as a last resort as they carry a limited quantity of five to six uses that requires 10 days to replenish. A skunk's first defense is to hiss and stamp its feet, followed by placing their tails high in the air. If you haven't gotten the message that you've upset the skunk and should run at this point, be prepared to get doused with skunk odor.

A Few Skunk Jokes (that truly stink):

Baby Skunk: "Mother, can I have a chemistry set?"

Mother Skunk: "What! And smell up the house?"

There were two skunks, one named In and one named Out. Once, Out went in and said to Out, "Bring In in." So Out went out, got In, and they went in. Their mother was happy to see them. She asked Out, "How did you find In so fast?" And Out said, "Instincts."

Q: Where does a skunk sit in a church?

A: In a Pew

Mountain Lion (*Puma concolor*)

Conservation Status: Least Concern

Description: Cougar, puma, mountain lion and catamount are all synonymous names for top predator of Henry Cowell Redwoods State Park. The mountain lion in general has the greatest range of any large terrestrial mammal in the Western Hemisphere and is found from the Yukon in Canada to the southern Andes of Chile. It is an adaptable animal and is found in every American habitat type. It is the second heaviest cat in the Western Hemisphere, the jaguar being the first. The mountain lion is a true carnivore, eating only meat.

The mountain lion is a nocturnal animal and uses a stalk and ambush method to attack its prey. It will typically prey on Mule Deer but has been known to attack domestic animals as well, such as cattle, horses and sheep. That being said, it is typically reclusive when it comes to humans and will avoid them under most circumstances. It is territorial, the size of which depending on the abundance of food within it. Besides eating large game, it also hunts rodents and even insects to augment a bigger catch.

Bobcat (*Felis rufus*)

Conservation Status: Least Concern

Description: Bobcats are the smallest of four species of medium sized wildcats referred to as lynxes. It is an adaptable predator found throughout the United States. It can be found primarily in the forested areas of Henry Cowell Redwoods State Park. They are solitary, able hunters, using a spotted coat as camouflage. It feeds mainly on rabbits and hares but will not pass by smaller prey such as insects or small rodents. Like the skunk, bobcat's hunt mainly at dusk and dawn. There have been reported cases of bobcats successfully killing larger animals such as deer.

Mating among the bobcats is a pursuit of the male. During courtship, the pair may undertake a number of different behaviors, such as bumping, chasing and ambushing as well as screams and hisses. The female will raise the young of one to six pups by herself after about 60 days of gestation. The pups are born with eyes closed, opening them after ten days. They begin exploring their surroundings at four weeks and within five months will accompany their mother on hunts. They will begin to hunt on their own by the fall of their first year.

In Henry Cowell, the cougar and coyote are the bobcats only known predator. However outside the park, bobcats are regularly hunted. Despite this, their numbers have remained steadily resilient.

Hoofed Animals (Artiodactyla)

Mule Deer (*Odocoileus hemionus*)

Conservation Status: Least Concern

Description: Mule Deer, including the California Mule Deer, are quite common and easily spotted by viewing their white rump with a black tip. They range from Mexico to Alaska and as far east as the Rocky Mountains. Most will be found foraging around dawn and dusk but may also forage during the full moon. They are known to bed down in the same area or in temporary beds. Repeated beds will be often scratched level and are about the size of a washtub. Temporary beds are more easily spotted as multiple flattened grassy areas. Mule deer rarely stray far from either water or forage and bed down within easy walking distance of both.

Young forage in groups while mature bucks travel alone or with other bucks. Mule deer are herbivores, and eat seasonally available plants. They will eat most woody vegetation, including Douglas fir, but little grass. In season they will eat acorns and wild berries.

Top predators beyond humans are mountain lions, coyotes and where present black bears. They have little defense mechanisms and rely almost exclusively on speed and alertness to avoid predation. The top two enemies of deer involve human interaction, hunting and automobiles.

No Longer Present

California Golden Bear, California Grizzly (*Ursus arctos horribilis*)

Conservation Status: Extinct in California, Threatened nationally

Description: Grizzly bears enjoyed a range from Alaska to Mexico and as far east as Hudson Bay. Today, the grizzly is only found in Alaska, Montana, Wyoming and occasionally in Canada. Ironically, the grizzly bear is the principle figure of the California State flag. The last known grizzly in this state was shot in 1922 by a rancher in Fresno.

Prior to human intrusion into the grizzly's range, the bear thrived in valleys and coastal slopes of California. Some researchers conclude that the grizzly was more abundant in California than any other state. By 1850 however, the California population exploded from 1,500 residents to 300,000, due exclusively to the Gold Rush. The gold miners both respected the grizzly and found them to be a threatening nuisance. In California as well as other states that grew in population, the grizzlies and civilization did not mix well. Unlike other mammals that faced similar threats from humans, grizzlies stood their ground and defended their territory rather than running to safer ground. This was a reasonable assumption as prior to humans, they were the top of the food chain, but it would prove to become a costly trait for the grizzly. Within 75 years of the Gold Rush, every grizzly would be hunted and killed or otherwise fled the state.

Pronghorn (*Antilocapra var.*)

Conservation Status: Limited in California, no longer present in Henry Cowell, Least Concern nationally

At one point, there were five species of pronghorn when humans first entered North America, now all but one, *A. Americana* is extinct. The pronghorn were one of the hunted animals of the Ohlone Native Americans. Today, pronghorn can be found in the northeast corner of California and in small to large pockets throughout the western United States.

Pronghorns are a migratory animal whose paths have been pinched off as humans inhabited them. As migration corridors were cut off, the pronghorn suffered as a result. As well, the pronghorn was actively hunted. In the 1920's the population was hunted to near extinction with only 13,000 animals left. Today, through both habitat protection and hunting restrictions, their numbers are closer to 500,000 to 1,000,000. Still habitat fragmentation will likely keep the pronghorn from returning to the park in the near future.

Closing Remarks

The purpose of these guide books is to connect the reader more deeply with the park they are visiting. Sometimes that is done by bringing in information that is directly related to the park, at times inserting a related topic that is only obliquely related and at other times it is by injecting a little humor at an unexpected moment. Whatever the method, I am truly fascinated at how deep and rich every State Park is within California. For me, learning that this was where Andrew P Hill had the epiphany to create the State Park was eye opening. This land is where it all began for the 279 some odd parks in California.

Perhaps the hardest piece to write in this book was on Isaac Graham. Historians have not been kind to the man, nor were many folks that knew him while he was alive. Even the plaque near his gravestone states that many were his friend because they feared his rifle. Yet, here was the man who arguably started the Mexican American conflicts with the Siege of Monterey. Here was the man who started the first water powered saw mill in the state. He was on one hand a respecting historical figure, a pioneer of California and the other hand a bad tempered misanthropic malcontent. Isaac Graham was a complicated person and it became a challenged topic to relay in an objective light. I kept asking myself what Isaac would think of what I wrote, if it had enough sinew mixed in with the respect due.

Then there is the park itself. Walk on any trail during a winter storm and you will feel the park consume all of your senses. Each breath feels pure, the scents of redwood on the tip of your nose, the sound of large drops circling you, the sheen of bark and rock and the needles under your feet; all of it tunes the mind, filling it with harmony and wonder. The park is both accessible and remote, it can be at times rugged and at others serene, but it is always welcoming to the visitor.

Take care, God bless and most of all thanks! ~ Eric Henze

About the Author

Eric Henze began his writing career at the age of twelve with a sci fi short titled "5:15", tackling a plot around a timepiece that could end the world. His passion for hiking started in Sedona, Arizona where he lived in his youth. It expanded to peak bagging in the Sierra Nevada Mountains and then the Andes of South America, where he lived as a Peace Corp volunteer for two years, climbing many of the peaks of Ecuador and Peru. A highlight was climbing Sangay, an active volcano that often shoots VW size rocks at climbers to maintain their attention. In his own words, "It was a delight".

His passions for writing, hiking and adventure have led to a series of guidebooks for both the National Park Service and the California State Parks. A portion of the proceeds of all of his books go towards directly supporting these parks. His latest work is titled "A Family Guide to the Grand Circle National Parks", a family oriented travel guide for seven national parks in the Southwestern United States.

Selected Reading

General

- The Complete Guide to Wilder Ranch State Park, by Eric Henze: http://www.amazon.com/Complete-Guide-Wilder-Ranch-State/dp/0989039218/
- Henry Cowell Redwwods State Park - Official Site: http://www.parks.ca.gov/?page_id=546
- Mountain Parks Foundation, the non profit that acts as the heart of Henry Cowell and other state parks: http://www.mountainparks.org/
- Friends of Santa Cruz website features much information on the parks and beaches of Santa Cruz: http://www.thatsmypark.org/
- Santa Cruz Bird Club website has tons of birding information for the Santa Cruz region: http://www.santacruzbirdclub.org/
- Lime Kiln Legacies is both a website and book devoted to Santa Cruz's lime kiln industry: http://limekilnlegacies.com/
- Swimming Holes of California: http://www.swimmingholes.org/ca.html
- The Outdoor Parent: http://www.theoutdoorparent.com/

Rancho Rincon:

- Ogden Hoffman, 1862, Reports of Land Cases Determined in the United States District Court for the Northern District of California, Numa Hubert, San Francisco
- Pinney, Thomas. 1989 A History of Wine in America: From the Beginnings to Prohibition. Berkeley: University of California Press, c1989
- Charles L. Sullivan, 1998, A Companion to California Wine: An Encyclopedia of Wine and Winemaking from the Mission Period to the Present, University of California Press,
- Who was Henry Cowell? : http://www.parks.ca.gov/?page_id=918
- Davis v. California Powder Works, 1890, Reports of Cases determined in the Supreme Court of the State of California, 84 Cal. 617, Volume 84, pp.617-634, Bancroft-Whitney Company
- Don Pedro Recreation Agency (2010). "Who was Don Pedro?". donpedrolake.com. Retrieved June 5, 2010.
- William Henry Ellison, 1950, A self-governing dominion, California, 1849-1860, University of California Press
- Eugene T Sawyer, 1922, History of Santa Clara County California

Rancho Zayante

- Diseño del Rancho Zayante: http://content.cdlib.org/ark:/13030/hb4r29n8xp/?
- Diseño del Rancho San Agustin: http://content.cdlib.org/ark:/13030/hb9w1008nv/?
- Donald Thomas Clark, Santa Cruz County Place Names: A Geographical Dictionary.
- Ogden Hoffman, 1862, Reports of Land Cases Determined in the United States District Court

- for the Northern District of California, Numa Hubert, San Francisco
- Rancho Zayante: http://www.parks.ca.gov/?page_id=913
- 3. Hoover, Mildred B.; Hero & Ethel Rensch, and William N. Abeloe (1966). Historic Spots in California. Stanford University Press.
- Pioneer Spirit: A History of the Winterhalder Family in Santa Cruz County by Geoffrey Dunn: http://www.santacruzpl.org/history/articles/247/
- Rafael Castro's Rancho Aptos was Oldest Land Grant to Remain Under Mexican Ownership by Jim Johnson: http://www.santacruzpl.org/history/articles/402/
- Death Valley in '49 / Manly, William Lewis: http://www.gutenberg.org/ebooks/12236
- Hiram Scott Profile by Jillian K. Duggan
- Asabel and Sarah Bennett, Emigrant Profile : http://www.octa-trails.org/search/asabel--sarah-bennett

Rancho Carbonera

- A Case Study of a Piracy Charge against Captain William Buckle By Victoria Creed Ph. D., Waihona Aina Corp. and Isaaca Hanson, a Leoiki/Buckle descendant: http://www.waihona.com/BucklePiracyCharges.html
- Scrimshaw in the New Bedford Whaling Museum By Stuart M. Frank
- Ogden Hoffman, 1862, Reports of Land Cases Determined in the United States District Court for the Northern District of California, Numa Hubert, San Francisco
- Rancho Carbonera: http://www.parks.ca.gov/?page_id=914

California Powder Works

- California Powder Works Santa Cruz Public Library Local History Articles: http://www.santacruzpl.org/history/articles/11/
- The California Powder Works & San Lorenzo Paper Mill by Barry Brown: http://www.santacruzpl.org/history/articles/508/

Captain Isaac Graham

- Captain Isaac Graham by Michael F. Kinsella:: http://sptddog.com/sotp/isaac1.html
- John F. Dye – Biography, The Museum of Art & History: http://researchforum.santacruzmah.org/viewtopic.php?t=112

Henry Cowell:

- Henry Cowell and His Family (1819--1955): Introduction by Laurie MacDougall: http://www.santacruzpl.org/history/articles/210/
- Cowell v Industrial Acc. Com.: http://scocal.stanford.edu/opinion/cowell-v-industrial-acc-com-28946
- University of California Chronicle, Volume 17
- About Wrentham: http://wrentham.ma.us/about-wrentham-ma-town
- UCSC Myth Breaker, The Cowell Ghost: http://ucscmyths.blogspot.com/2008/10/cowell-ghost.html

Welchs Big Tree Grove

- The San Lorenzo Valley by Lisa Robinson
- Santa Cruz Trains: Big Trees Station: http://www.santacruztrains.com/2012/05/big-trees-station.html
- Andrew P. Hill Sempervirens : http://sempervirens.org/about-us/our-history/
- The Valley of Heart's Delight, Andrew P. Hill: http://www.mariposaresearch.net/santaclararesearch/SCBIOS/aphill.html
- Hill Award for Inspiration: http://www.parks.ca.gov/pages/23071/files/2_hillaward_flyer2007.pdf

John Frémont

- John C. Frémont: http://en.wikipedia.org/wiki/John_C._Fr%C3%A9mont

Photo Attributes

Attributions and permissions given where indicated.

Cover Photos
- All photos front and back by author

Title Page
- Fall Creek, by author

In order of appearance.

General Information
- Parking: Imagery©2013 AMBAG, DigitalGlobe, GeoEye, USDA Farm Service Agency, Map data ©2013 Google
- Redwood sorrel flower, by Eric Henze
- Henry Cowell Campground, by Eric Henze
- Henry Cowell Fee Sign, by Eric Henze
- Fall Creek, by Eric Henze
- Bench near Lime Kilns, by Eric Henze
- Turkey Tail Mushroom, by Eric Henze

Area History
- Mission San Jose Natives, from Mission San Juan Capistrano: A Pocket History and Tour Guide, PD - US
- Ohlone Tule Huts, unknown, CC-PD-Mark
- Ohlone Tribe Building Mission, unknown, CC-PD-Mark
- Entrevue de l'expedition de M. Kotzebue avec le roi Tammeamea dans l'ile d'Ovayhi, Iles Sandwich, by Louis Choris (1795-1828), CC-PD-Mark
- Sainsevain Brothers listing Sainsevain's California Wine Bitters, 1862 San Francisco City Directory, CC-PD-Mark
- California Powder Works Bridge, by permission of the John Carney Family Collection
- Captain Isaac Graham, Scenes of Wonder & Curiosity from Hutchings' California Magazine, 1856-1861, CC-PD-Mark
- Isaac Graham in Indian Fight, Scenes of Wonder & Curiosity from Hutchings' California Magazine, 1856-1861, CC-PD-Mark
- Isaac Graham as a Trapper, Scenes of Wonder & Curiosity from Hutchings' California Magazine, 1856-1861, CC-PD-Mark
- Storming Isaac's House, Scenes of Wonder & Curiosity from Hutchings' California Magazine, 1856-1861, CC-PD-Mark
- Monterey Jail, Scenes of Wonder & Curiosity from Hutchings' California Magazine, 1856-1861, CC-PD-Mark
- Road to Tepic, Scenes of Wonder & Curiosity from Hutchings' California Magazine, 1856-1861, CC-PD-Mark
- Tilatha Catherine Bennett (1824-1880), CC-PD-Mark
- Henry Cowell, by permission of the S.H. Cowell Foundation
- Lime Workers, by permission of the S.H. Cowell Foundation
- Cowell Lime Works, ca 1889, by permission of the S.H. Cowell Foundation
- Loading Lime onto ship, by permission of the S.H. Cowell Foundation
- Henry Cowell in front of the carriage house at the Cowell Ranch, late 1800's, by permission of the S.H. Cowell Foundation
- Two of the three Cowell sisters, by permission of the S.H. Cowell Foundation
- Samuel Harry Cowell, by permission of the S.H. Cowell Foundation
- Cowell Lime works ca 1962, Ansel Adams, by permission of the S.H. Cowell Foundation
- Big Trees Postcard, CC-PD-Mark

- Portrait of Andrew Putnam Hill in 1900, age 45 (History San Jose), CC-PD-Mark
- Original Sempervirens Club members, 1900, by A. P. Hill (History San Jose), CC-PD-Mark
- Postcard, Welch's Calling Card Tree, CC-PD-Mark
- Picture of John Charles Frémont, 1852, PD-OLD
- Postcard, Fremont in front of Fremont Tree, CC-PD-Mark

Geology
- Santa Cruz Sand Hills, by Eric Henze

Trails in the Main Unit
- All photos by author

Trails in the Fall Creek Unit
- All photos by author

Flora
- Arctostaphylos silvicola Ghostly Manzanita, by permission of laspilitas.com
- Arctostaphylos silvicola Ghostly Manzanita, by permission of laspilitas.com
- Close up of a Pinus attenuata cone (11.5 cm long, by Geographer, CC-BY-2.5
- Mimulus aurantiacus — Sticky Monkey-flower, by Geographer, CC-BY-1.0
- A Bay Checkerspot Butterfly (Euphydryas editha bayensis), by Fcb981, CC-BY-SA-3.0-migrated
- Ceanothus papillosus, by Stan Shebs, CC-BY-SA-3.0
- Ceanothus papillosus, by Stan Shebs, CC-BY-SA-3.0
- Pinus ponderosa, by Mitch, CC-BY-SA-2.0
- Dendromecon rigida — Bush poppy, by NPS employee, PD US NPS
- Pacific Madrone (Arbutus menziesii) blossom, by Seglea, PD-user
- Pale Swallowtail, Papilio eurymedon, by Franco Folini, CC-BY-SA-3.0-migrated
- Pteridium aquilinum, by Rasbak, CC-BY-SA-3.0-migrated
- Diffuse Spineflower, by unknown, PD-User
- Crocanthemum scoparium, by Unknown, PD US NPS
- Acer negundo, by USDA employee, PD USDA
- Salix lasiolepis, by William & Wilma Follette, PD USDA
- Salix lasiolepis, by unknown, PD-User
- Big Leaf Maple, Tony Perodeau, by PD-user
- Black Cottonwood (Populus trichocarpa), by Walter Siegmund, CC-BY-SA-3.0-migrated
- Trunk of a large cottonwood tree, by Beeblebrox, CC-BY-SA-3.0
- Alnus rhombifolia, by NPS employee, PD US NPS
- Bare Platanus racemosa, Downtowngal, CC-BY-SA-3.0
- Rhododendron occidentale, by Eric Hunt, CC-BY-SA-3.0-migrated
- Dicentra bachanal, by Ramin Nakisa, CC-BY-SA-3.0-migrated-with-disclaimers
- Viola adunca, Thegreenj, CC-BY-SA-3.0-migrated
- Trillium chloropetalum rubrum, Ramin Nakisa, CC-BY-SA-3.0-migrated-with-disclaimers
- Lithocarpus densiflorus leaves, by Joseph O'Brien, CC-BY-3.0-US
- Pacific Madrone (Arbutus menziesii), by NaJina McEnany, CC-BY-SA-2.5
- Pacific Madrone (Arbutus menziesii) blossom, by Stephen Lea, PD-user
- Archibald Menzies (1754-1842), PD Old
- Coast Douglas-fir, by Cruiser, CC-BY-3.0
- Redwoods, unknown, PD-self
- Umbellularia californica — California Bay Laurel, by employee of USG, PD US Government
- A spring twig of Interior Live Oak with an acorn, by Benny White, CC-BY-SA-3.0
- Poison Oak, by Elf, CC-BY-SA-3.0-migrated-with-disclaimers
- Poison Oak green phase, by Leonard G.., CC-SA-1.0
- Poison Oak red phase, by Leonard G.., CC-SA-1.0
- Western Sword Fern, by Jami Dwyer, CC-BY-SA-2.0
- Corylus cornuta, by unknown, PD US Government
- Woodwardia fimbriata, Anthony Valois, PD US NPS
- Pacific Trillium, by Walter Siegmund, CC-BY-SA-3.0,2.5,2.0,1.0

- Fetid Adder's Tongue, Eric in SF, CC-BY-SA-3.0
- Pacific Hound's Tongue, Grand Hound's Tongue, Walter Siegmund, CC-BY-SA-3.0,2.5,2.0,1.0
- Milkmaids, by Elf, CC-BY-SA-3.0-migrated
- Redwood Sorrel (Oxalis oregana), Walter Siegmund, CC-BY-SA-3.0-migrated
- Baccharis pilularis (coyote brush), by Evangele19, CC-BY-SA-3.0
- Rubus armeniacus, by Forest & Kim Starr, CC-BY-3.0
- Avena fatua, by Kurt Stueber, CC-BY-SA-3.0-migrated
- Beardless Wild Rye, Robert H. Mohlenbrock, PD US Government
- California poppy (Eschscholzia californica californica), by Kaldari, CC-Zero
- Madia elegans, by Noah Elhardt, CC-BY-SA-2.5
- Shooting star (Dodecatheon clevelandii), by unknown, PD-User
- Chlorogalum pomeridianum, by Tom Hilton, CC-BY-2.0
- Purple owl's clover, by Calibas, CC-BY-SA-4.0,3.0,2.5,2.0,1.0
- Vetch, by unknown, CC-BY-SA-3.0-migrated
- Cow parsnip leaf, by Danielle Langlois, CC-BY-SA-3.0-migrated
- Cow parsnip flowers, by Danielle Langlois, CC-BY-SA-3.0-migrated

Fauna

- Steelhead Oncorhynchus mykiss, Scanned from plates in Evermann, Barton Warren; Goldsborough, Edmund Lee (1907) The Fishes of Alaska, by A Hoen and Co., PD US Government
- A rough-skinned newt, by Jsayre64, CC-BY-SA-3.0
- Picture of a banana slug taken on the campus of UC Santa Cruz, by Jim Whitehead, CC-BY-2.0
- Virginia Opossum (Didelphis virginiana), by Wilson44691, PD-self
- Mole hand. by Nova, CC-BY-SA-3.0-migrated
- American Shrew Mole, by USDA employee, PD US USDA FS
- Scapanus latimanus, by Sarah Murray, CC-BY-SA-2.0
- Big eared townsend bat (Corynorhinus townsendii), exact author unknown, PD US GOV
- Brush Rabbit (Sylvilagus bachmani), by Walter Siegmund, CC-BY-SA-3.0-migrated
- Desert Cottontail (Sylvilagus audubonii), by Howcheng, CC-BY-SA-3.0
- Photo of a black-tailed jackrabbit, by Jim Harper, CC-BY-SA-2.5
- Neotamias merriami, Merriam's Chipmunk, by Greg Schechter, CC-BY-2.0
- California Ground Squirrel (Spermophilus beecheyi), by Howcheng, CC-BY-SA-3.0
- Western Gray Squirrel, by unknown, CC-BY-3.0
- Pocket Gopher, by Leonardo Weiss, CC-BY-3.0
- Dipodomys ordii, by unknown, PD US Government
- Captive bred Peromyscus maniculatus (Deer Mouse), by 6th Hapiness, CC-BY-SA-3.0
- Adult female Neotoma fuscipes, Mbmceach, CC-BY-SA-3.0
- Woodrat house/den at Stebbins Cold Creek Canyon, CA, Mbmceach, CC-BY-SA-3.0
- A Black Rat, by Kilessan, CC-BY-SA-3.0
- Dance of Death, by Michael Wolgemut (1493), PD-Art (PD-old-100)
- Microtus californicus, Jerry Kirkhart, CC-BY-2.0
- Canis latrans, by Christopher Bruno, CC-BY-SA-3.0-migrated
- Gray Fox (Urocyon cinereoargenteus), by Gary M. Stolz, PD US FWS
- Raccoon, by Darkone, CC-BY-SA-2.5
- Long-tailed Weasel, by Joern Hauke, CC-BY-SA-3.0
- Striped Skunks (Mephitis mephitis), www.birdphotos.com, CC-BY-3.0
- Striped Skunk, by Jef Poskanzer, CC-BY-2.0
- Mountain Lion, by unknown, PD
- Paw of a puma, by MichaTP, CC-BY-3.0
- Bobcat (Lynx rufus), by Calibas, PD-self
- Mule deer (Odocoileus hemionus), by Tupper Ansel Blake, PD US FWS
- Brown Bear, by Jon Nickles, PD US Government
- Pair of pronghorn (Antilocapra americana), by Samsara, CC-BY-SA-2.0

Attributes

- The Open Invitation, by Author

www.ingramcontent.com/pod-product-compliance
Lightning Source LLC
Chambersburg PA
CBHW050636300426
44112CB00012B/1825